The Effective Parent

Other Works by the Authors

The Parent's Handbook: Systematic Training for Effective
   Parenting (Don Dinkmeyer and Gary D. McKay)

The Parent's Guide: Systematic Training for Effective
   Parenting of Teens (Don Dinkmeyer and Gary D. McKay)

PREP for Effective Family Living (Don Dinkmeyer, Gary D. McKay,
   Don Dinkmeyer, Jr., James S. Dinkmeyer, and Jon Carlson)

Time for a Better Marriage (Don Dinkmeyer and Jon Carlson)

Raising a Responsible Child (Don Dinkmeyer and Gary D. McKay)

The Encouragement Book (Don Dinkmeyer and Lewis E. Losoncy)

The Effective Parent

Don Dinkmeyer
Gary D. McKay
Don Dinkmeyer, Jr.
James S. Dinkmeyer
Joyce L. McKay

AGS® American Guidance Service • Circle Pines, Minnesota 55014-1796

AGS staff participating in the development and production of this publication:

PROJECT TEAM
Flora Taylor, Project Editor
Leslie Pfaff, Mary Kaye Kuzma, Production Coordinators
Bud Moravetz, Marketing Associate

PROGRAM DIVISION
Dorothy Chapman, Director
Lois Welshons, Art Editor
Bonnie Goldsmith, Senior Editor

SUPPORT SERVICES
David Youngquist, Director
Julie Nauman Peters, Graphic Designer
Carol McLean, Lynne Cromwell, Production Managers
Sylvia Carsen, Production Artist
Maureen Wilson, Art Director

Cartoons by John Bush

Printed in the United States of America.

A   10   9   8   7   6   5

Library of Congress Catalog Card Number: 86-72464

ISBN 0-913476-68-4

To the parents and leaders of *STEP* and *STEP/Teen,*
for their investment in children.

Contents

Introduction ix

Chapter 1 Taking a Fresh Look at Your Parenting 1

Chapter 2 Building Self-Esteem 27

Chapter 3 How Lifestyle Beliefs Affect Your Parenting 51

Chapter 4 Stress: Coping with Changes and Challenges 77

Chapter 5 Making Decisions as a Family 103

Chapter 6 Gentle Strength and Firm Love 125

Appendix Review of *STEP* Principles 149

Group Discussion Programs — More Help for Becoming an Effective Parent 163

Skill Cards 167

Introduction

Today's concerned parents often turn to parent education programs for help with the challenges they face. Down-to-earth, practical principles form the basis of two of the most widely used parent education programs in the world, *STEP (Systematic Training for Effective Parenting)* and *STEP/Teen.* In these programs, parents learn skills for understanding and dealing with children's behavior more effectively. If you've taken a *STEP* or *STEP/Teen* course, your family relationships may have improved dramatically—yet you may still lack confidence in your parenting, or feel uncertain at times about how and when to apply the skills you've learned. By inviting you to take an in-depth look at yourself as a parent, this book, *The Effective Parent,* takes you a step further in developing the skills and confidence you need to meet the challenges of family living.

Whether or not you're a graduate of one of the *STEP* programs, you will find that *The Effective Parent* has something important to offer you. You'll learn ways to build your own and your children's self-esteem. You'll explore how your beliefs and attitudes affect your parenting and learn how you can build on your strengths to have a more positive impact on the lives of your children. You'll find specific strategies for dealing with stress, suggestions for strengthening your family's decision-making process, and guidelines for asserting your rights as a parent without abandoning the democratic approach. You'll be encouraged to participate in group problem solving, learning to give and receive feedback on individual parenting concerns. You'll find valuable information applicable to all family structures.

This book assumes some familiarity with the basic principles of *STEP*—the goals of misbehavior, positive goals of behavior, family constellation, problem ownership, reflective listening, I-messages, and natural and logical consequences. If it's been a while since you studied these concepts, or if you're new to the *STEP* approach, you may want to begin by reading through the appendix at the back of this book, "Review of *STEP* Principles."

To gain the maximum benefit from this book, we suggest that you read each chapter carefully and use the concluding Family Enrichment Activity and Activity for the Week to put the principles into practice in your family. In the back of the book you will find tear-out cards that reinforce what you are learning. These Skill Cards help you quickly locate information specific to important skills. For example, several of the cards contain directions for relaxation exercises. The cards are a convenient size to carry with you for reference.

The Effective Parent is the participant's book for a discussion program that's a follow-up to *STEP* and *STEP/Teen*. It's called *The Next STEP: Effective Parenting through Problem Solving*. We encourage you to join or form a *Next STEP* group. There you'll meet with a group leader and other parents to discuss the ideas in this book and to help each other with specific parenting challenges. Turn to page 163 for more information about parent groups and about *The Next STEP*.

Whether you're studying this book on your own or participating in a group, we wish you a successful parenting experience. We invite you to join—or renew your membership in—the *STEP* family, parents who rely on *STEP* principles and practices as they enjoy satisfying relationships with their children.

Don Dinkmeyer, Ph.D.
President, Communication and Motivation Training Institute, Inc. (CMTI), Coral Springs, Florida
Diplomate of Counseling Psychology, American Board of Professional Psychology
Diplomate, American Board of Family Psychology
Clinical Member, American Association for Marriage and Family Therapy

Gary D. McKay, Ph.D.
President, Communication and Motivation Training Institute-West, Inc. (CMTI-West), Tucson, Arizona
Educational and Psychological Consultant
Clinical Member, American Association for Marriage and Family Therapy

Don Dinkmeyer, Jr., Ph.D.
Editor, CMTI Press
President, North American Society of Adlerian Psychology

James S. Dinkmeyer, M.A.
Associate, CMTI
Counselor and Consultant

Joyce L. McKay, Ph.D.
Vice-President, CMTI-West
Counselor and Consultant

CHAPTER ONE

Taking a
Fresh Look at
Your Parenting

What Is Effective Parenting?

Remember when your children were infants? You had to do *everything* for them. They depended on you for survival itself. The responsibilities you faced may have seemed overwhelming. Perhaps you comforted yourself by saying, "Soon they'll be older."

But as your children grew and developed, they presented new parenting challenges. You may have responded by continuing to try to do everything for them—giving in to their demands, feeling guilty about saying no—until you felt more like a slave than a parent. Or you may have tried to control their behavior by using rewards and punishments or demanding obedience. You meant well; you were concerned. You wanted to be a "good" parent and to have well-behaved children who would grow up to be happy, successful adults. But parenthood probably felt like quite a burden!

Perhaps at that point you sought help. Along with many other parents, you may have discovered *Systematic Training for Effective Parenting.* If you've taken a *STEP* or *STEP/Teen* course,* you've learned that we can't wait until our children reach adulthood to begin transferring responsibility to them. Children become adults by learning to accept increasing responsibility for themselves and their actions. It can be a relief to realize that your job is not to control your children or to do things *for* them, but simply to teach responsibility. To do that, an effective parent

- sets limits
- permits choices

*See the Introduction to this book for details about *STEP* and *STEP/Teen* programs.

- focuses on possibilities and solutions
- notices progress and improvement
- respects children and accepts them as they are
- doesn't blame or criticize children
- allows children to own their own problems
- permits children to make their own decisions when appropriate
- lets children experience the consequences of their decisions

Once parents learn these *STEP* principles, they are eager to apply them. But sometimes they run into difficulties.

Falling Back into Ineffective Patterns

In day-to-day dealings with their children, parents often face tough decisions. It's natural to feel uncertain what's best at times. And it's easy to slip back into old patterns, as the following examples show:

Josephine learned in her STEP/Teen *class that nagging her daughter Belinda to study was keeping her from learning to take responsibility for her own schoolwork. So Josephine stepped aside for a time in order to let Belinda have the experience of receiving poor grades as a logical consequence of her poor study habits.* But when Belinda brought home a report card with D's and F's, the following scene took place:*

Josephine: *[triumphantly] Look at these grades! I guess this will be a lesson to you—you'll have to really buckle down and study now if you expect to graduate this year.*

Belinda: *Do you think I care what grades I get? Nag, nag, nag—that's all you ever do. I'm not going to study and you can't make me!*

---

*See the appendix, "Review of *STEP* Principles," for an explanation of natural and logical consequences.

Josephine: That does it! I'm grounding you for the next two weeks. We'll see who's in charge here!

Josephine started out with the intention of letting Belinda accept responsibility for her own academic work. But now Josephine is plunging into a power struggle.

Andrea's son Jonah wasn't getting along well with his fifth grade teacher. Andrea learned in her STEP class that it would be best to let Jonah work out the problem with his teacher on his own. So Andrea made a point of not going to see the teacher. But when Jonah came home unhappy and complained that the teacher was picking on him, Andrea sympathized with him. She gave him treats after school to comfort him, and sometimes she helped him with his home-work so he'd be able to make a good impression on the teacher.

Andrea's original intention was not to interfere in Jonah's relationship with his teacher. But without realizing it, that's exactly what she's doing!

Rodrigo's son Felipe, age seven, was also having trouble at school. His teacher wrote that Felipe was withdrawn and seemed to lack self-confidence. Rodrigo learned in a PECES course* that he needed to give Felipe more encouragement. So when Felipe brought home a picture he'd drawn at school one day, Rodrigo went out of his way to take time to admire it. It was colorful and filled with lively details. "I see you've used a lot of color and taken a lot of time," he told Felipe. "Of course, the chimney on the house could be a lit-tle bit straighter."

By adding a critical remark to his positive statement, Rodrigo is actually discouraging Felipe.

Herman's daughter Kay was just starting to date. Herman had realized from taking a STEP/Teen course that if he wanted a curfew to be effective, he would have to set up log-ical consequences for coming home late. The first time Kay broke her curfew, this is what happened:

---

*PECES (Padres Eficaces Con Entrenamiento Sistemático)
is a Spanish-language edition of *STEP.*

Herman: Kay, I told you that if you came home late you'd be grounded for a week. Consider yourself grounded.

Kay: Oh, Daddy, it wasn't my fault—my watch stopped! Besides, I was only forty-five minutes late. Don't you trust me? If you ground me, I'll miss Roger's party! Everybody who's anybody will be there. If you don't let me go to Roger's party my social life will be ruined! [Kay bursts into tears.]

Herman: [To himself] I guess she's got a point—how can she learn to handle responsibility if I don't show her I trust her? And I can't bear to see her so unhappy. [Out loud] Well, I guess we could make an exception this time, since this party is so special to you.

Despite his good intentions, Herman is teaching Kay to be irresponsible.

These parents, all well-meaning, have gone astray because they are acting on mistaken beliefs.

What Are Mistaken Beliefs?

If you've had a *STEP* course, you'll recall that children misbehave because they are discouraged and feel they don't belong. The misbehavior of younger children has one of four basic goals: attention, power, revenge, or display of inadequacy. These goals of misbehavior come from mistaken beliefs:

- "I must be the center of attention."

- "I don't count unless I get things my way."

- "Since people have hurt me and don't love me—since I am unlovable—the only way I can get any response from others is by hurting them."

- "I am inadequate."

Teens may also misbehave with the goals of attention, power, revenge, or display of inadequacy. But teen misbehavior may have other goals: excitement, peer acceptance,

The Goals of Misbehavior Come from Mistaken Beliefs

or superiority. Teens sometimes mistakenly believe that,

- "In order to make my life exciting, I must use alcohol or other drugs, engage in sex, participate in daredevil sports . . ."
- "I must have the approval of my peers."
- "I must be the best."*

Like younger children and teens, parents also sometimes base their actions on mistaken beliefs they are unaware of. Some common mistaken beliefs that can interfere with using the *STEP* approach effectively are

- "I must be in control."
- "I am superior."
- "I must be perfect."
- "I must please others."

"I must be in control." Parents who believe "I must be in control" or "I'm always right" often do not let their children experience natural and logical consequences. These parents will have a tendency to interfere, argue, or attempt to show who's the boss—like Josephine. Their children may be inclined to rebel, seek revenge, give up, or become evasive. Caught up in reacting against a controlling parent, a child may have trouble developing true independence and self-discipline.

"I am superior." Parents who spoil their children or interfere, who pity them or try to overprotect them, may be acting on the belief "I am superior." Can you recognize Andrea in this description? The children of "superior" parents may feel inadequate or learn to blame and criticize others. Like their parents, they may end up believing they are better than other people. These children are likely to learn self-pity.

---

*For further discussion of the goals of misbehavior, see the appendix.

"I must be perfect." Parents who believe "I must be perfect" usually demand perfection from others. By calling attention to what he sees as a flaw in Felipe's drawing, that's what Rodrigo is doing. The children of "perfect" parents may feel that nothing they do is ever good enough. They may become perfectionists themselves—or they may give up. They frequently get discouraged and are likely to worry too much about what other people think.

"I must please others." When parents act on the belief "I don't count" or "I must please others," they teach their children to expect others to give in to them and to wait on them. The children may be selfish and have poor social relationships as a result. Herman's wish to please Kay is likely to have undesirable results.

Our mistaken beliefs don't just affect our children. We get discouraged ourselves at not being able to live up to these beliefs. But understanding *why* we behave the way we do can lead to positive changes in our parenting.

Finding Fresh Perspectives

Identifying mistaken beliefs that may be influencing your parenting is the first step toward becoming a more effective parent. Your next step is to replace the unhelpful beliefs with more constructive ones.

Your view of the world influences how you experience everything that happens to you. Fortunately, there is always more than one way to look at any experience—perceptual alternatives always exist.[1] By choosing how you interpret events, you can find constructive ways to look at yourself, your life, and your relationships.

Understanding your children and their goals is important. But it's also important to understand yourself. You make up half the parent-child relationship. Often a shift in your own attitude or beliefs can make a big difference in the relationship.

Dom grew up listening to his father and keeping his opinions to himself. Now he has a son of his own, seventeen-year-old Frank. Frank often disagrees openly with Dom, who believes such behavior is disrespectful. His own father would never have stood for it! But when Dom took a STEP/Teen course, he began to realize how important it is for teens to begin to separate themselves from the family and develop their own opinions. His attitude toward Frank changed. He began to see Frank's independent thinking as a strength that would stand him in good stead once he reached adulthood.

As a result of this insight, Dom became more tolerant and started listening to what Frank had to say. Frank noticed the change. Once he began to feel that his father respected him, he became less aggressive and argumentative.

You can choose what meaning
you give to a situation.

Remembering that you can choose what meaning you give to a situation allows you to be flexible. Choosing to look at events in a new way can give you the perspective you need to solve your parenting problems.

Seeing Possibilities and Solutions

Most of us are skillful at noticing what's wrong with our own and others' behavior. But we can learn to shift our attention from the negative to the positive. We can choose to see possibilities and solutions rather than threats and dangers.

Anna May's son Gil wanted to go on an overnight bike trip with his best friend. Anna May was concerned about the hazards such a trip might hold for two thirteen-year-olds "You might get hurt in traffic," she told Gil. "And what if it rains? You could catch cold. And where would you camp? Those public campsites just aren't safe!"

But Gil persisted in wanting to go. In giving it further thought, Anna May realized that such a trip could help Gil develop more self-confidence and self-reliance. The boys could use the exercise and it would be nice for them to get out of the city for the weekend. But she was still concerned for their safety. They really needed adult supervision.

Then she remembered seeing in the paper that the YMCA had sponsored a bike tour recently. Maybe that was a possibility! Or she could call their scoutmaster—maybe he'd be willing to chaperone a group trip. Once she stopped focusing on the dangers and started looking for solutions, a lot of possibilities occurred to her, and she enlisted the boys' help in exploring them.

Choosing Constructive Attitudes

Looking for positive viewpoints doesn't mean we ignore the serious challenges that face us. A change of viewpoint won't make problems go away. But it *can* be the basis of an effec-

We can choose to notice people's good points.

tive approach for dealing with them. We can choose attitudes that will improve relationships and build self-esteem, attitudes that allow us to say,

- "It's okay to make mistakes."

- "Let's talk it over and see if we can't work something out."

- "I don't like what you did, but I still love you."

- "What you did today was unacceptable, but you can try again tomorrow."

In our contacts with others, we can be encouraging by choosing to notice and comment on their good points. We can also observe ourselves and take time to appreciate the good things we see. The encouragement we give ourselves and others builds confidence and feelings of worth.

Humor—Always A Helpful Ingredient

Humor is powerful. Whenever we can see humor in an event, our attention has shifted away from the event's discouraging aspects. We can put what has happened in perspective. We see more than the dark side of the situation.

Often we try to impose our standards on life rather than accepting life as it is. We tell ourselves "This is the way it should be" or "This is the way I should be." This limits us and separates us from a joyful, realistic view of life. Humor can help us break out of confining patterns and enjoy the present moment.

Suppose you return from the grocery store and discover you forgot to buy hamburger buns—the item you went to the store to get. You can choose how to react. You can put yourself down—"I'm so dumb. How could anybody be that stupid?" Or you can laugh—and go back to the store or change the menu.

Working with Others to Solve Parenting Problems

When mistaken beliefs come between a parent's understanding of a *STEP* concept and its direct application to the child, the parent's effectiveness is decreased. Since parents frequently are unaware of their beliefs, they may not understand why they are having difficulty. And if they do become aware of a mistaken belief, they may feel stuck with it. It isn't easy for people to come up with new ways of looking at things.

But by working together in groups, listening to one another carefully and offering support, parents can help each other identify and change unhelpful beliefs. Once parents discover how their belief systems are interfering, they can learn to apply *STEP* principles more effectively.*

What You Can Accomplish in a Problem-Solving Group

The problem-solving group is a powerful method of parent education. It offers a procedure for taking a systematic look at specific parenting problems. The group takes into consideration the child's behavior, the parent's feelings about it, and the parent's underlying thoughts and beliefs. Participants can apply all they have learned to each member's parenting challenges.

You can develop skill in identifying and applying the *STEP* concepts appropriate to a specific situation.

*See the Introduction for information on the availability of parenting groups based on this book.

As a group member, you can

- make the principles of human behavior learned in *STEP* and *STEP/Teen* a practical part of relationships with your children

- increase your understanding of the beliefs, motives, and feelings involved in conflicts with children

- develop skill in coming up with new and productive ways of looking at experiences

- develop skill in identifying and applying the *STEP* concepts appropriate to a specific situation

- learn to identify which situations you should try to change

- give and receive encouragement.

Steps in Problem Solving

1. Present your parenting problem to the group.

- Describe in detail a specific parenting challenge, telling exactly what your child did and said. Also describe what happened before the event and what followed it.

- Avoid generalizations—"My daughter is always lazy," "My son never minds me." Instead, tell about the most recent time your daughter acted lazy or your son refused to mind you. Tell the group what they need to know in order to visualize the situation accurately.

- Tell how you felt at the time about what happened. If it isn't clear how you were feeling, someone may ask, "How did you feel then (when your child did or said that)?"

- Having told what happened and how you felt about it, go on to explain what you said and did in response to the situation.

- Describe what you were telling yourself at the time. You may have been thinking "It's not fair," "I'm going to get even," "How can she treat me this way?" or "Nothing ever works anyway." This kind of internal dialogue can provide clues to your beliefs about parenting, about the relationship, and about how you are being treated.

- Describe what the child did in response to your action.

By this point, the group should have a clear picture of the transaction, including

> the child's behavior
>
> your feelings, actions, and thoughts
>
> the child's response

2. Let group members guess what the child's goal was in the situation described—attention, power, revenge, display of inadequacy, superiority, excitement, or peer acceptance.* Their conclusions will be tentative, and you have the right to accept or reject their ideas.

3. Ask the group if they've noticed any beliefs that may be interfering with your effectiveness.

4. With the help of the group, identify who owns the problem, your child or you.** Deciding who owns the problem helps greatly in determining what action is needed and appropriate.[2]

5. Brainstorm different ways of looking at the situation (perceptual alternatives). If you can see the situation in a

---

*Some guidelines for determining goals of misbehavior are provided in the appendix.

**For an explanation of how to decide who owns a problem, see the appendix.

Deciding who owns the problem
helps greatly in determining what action
is needed and appropriate.

new light, you will be less bound to the same old ways of responding. Group members can help each other find new perspectives by asking,

- "Is there another way of looking at this?"

- "What else might you have done?"

- "Is there something positive in the child's behavior? If so, how can it be encouraged?"

The group may be able to help you see a humorous side to your difficulties.

6. Continue brainstorming to find suggestions for improving the parent-child relationship. While your situation is being discussed, listen to all suggestions without judging them. You may feel like giving excuses or saying why what is being suggested will not work, but *your job at this point is just to listen.*

7. After hearing the group's suggestions, choose a specific course of action and tell why you chose it. If you feel none of the suggestions are appropriate, you can ask the group to brainstorm again. Or, you can ask that the discussion be tabled until the next session's problem-solving time.

If you do choose a course of action, make a commitment to stick with it until the next session. This commitment should be very specific. Say exactly what you will do and under what circumstances. It's helpful to put commitments in writing.

At the next group session, when the problem-solving segment begins, you will have a chance to share how things went during the week as you worked on your commitment. The group may take a few minutes to offer you additional suggestions.

Your Responsibilities as a Group Member

In order to make the group process meaningful and effective, it is essential to follow certain guidelines:

1. *Treat the other members of the group as your equals.* There are no perfect parents and no one has perfect children. Everyone has challenges and is entitled to ask for help with them. Everyone has something to contribute to brainstorming and the search for solutions. Everyone's full participation is needed.

2. *Keep a balance between providing and receiving help.* This helps ensure that each person will have an opportunity to be heard and to receive group feedback. Everyone needs to take responsibility for seeing that no one monopolizes the time.

3. *Keep information shared within the group confidential.* When you're outside the group, do not discuss anything that has come up in the problem-solving process, not even

Steps of Group Problem Solving

1. Present your parenting problem to the group:
   - Tell what your child did and how you felt about it.
   - Explain what you said and did in response to the child's behavior.
   - Tell what your thoughts were.
   - Describe what the child did in response to your words and action.

2. Let group members guess what the child's goal of misbehavior was.

3. Ask the group if they have spotted any mistaken beliefs on your part that may be interfering with your effectiveness.

4. With the help of the group, identify who owns the problem.

5. Brainstorm different ways of looking at the situation.

6. Continue brainstorming to find suggestions for improving the parent-child relationship.

7. Choose a specific course of action, explain why you chose it, and make a commitment to stick with it until the next session.

with other group members. Confidentiality lets members feel safe sharing their concerns and talking about their beliefs and attitudes.

4. *Make a commitment to change.* Recognize that this is more than a discussion group. This is also your chance to make changes with group support.

Creating the Right Atmosphere

The following factors help create an atmosphere in which open, honest, effective interaction can take place:

1. *Acceptance.* An accepting group member respects others in the group and always speaks to them respectfully. Imagining what it's like to be in the other person's shoes will put you into an accepting frame of mind. Make an active attempt to understand the dynamics of the other members' families—the problems involved, the belief systems, the feelings, and any obstacles to being the kind of parents they would like to be. Bear in mind that the other parents in your group have good intentions, even though you may spot faulty methods, misinformation, or mistaken beliefs.

2. *Feedback.* In order to learn how others see us, we need to know how our beliefs and behavior affect other people—we need feedback. Feedback should be based on mutual respect and caring. Give feedback honestly and openly, with the goal of helping. Don't demand that the other person change; just share your perceptions. Feedback is the most valuable gift another group member receives from you.

Before giving feedback to anyone, ask whether they feel ready to hear it. This gives them a choice and shows you respect them. It lets them know they aren't being attacked. Only go ahead with feedback when you have been given permission and feel it will be welcomed.

Another way to help make sure your feedback is not perceived as an attack is to state it in the form of an I-message, a statement expressing your own feelings: "When you were

Before giving feedback to anyone,
ask whether they feel ready to hear it.

explaining what you said to your son, I found myself feeling discouraged. I wonder if he feels the same way."*

Karen has given George permission to give her feedback. George proceeds by saying, "I'm not sure you're aware of how you sound when you're talking about your daughter. I sense anger in your voice. I wonder if your daughter hears it too." Note that George is using I-messages and presents his interpretation tentatively—"I'm not sure," "I sense," "I wonder." Karen is free to accept or reject what George has said.

Remember to give feedback that is encouraging. Take every opportunity to focus on a parent's strengths or to show that you have faith in someone's ability to change and grow.

*I-messages are explained in the appendix and discussed in Chapter 6.

3. *Universalization.* What happens in your family may seem unique, but through the group you will learn that others share your concerns and have similar parenting challenges. This is called universalization. When someone describes a situation, the leader may ask, "Has anyone else had that concern?" You will find that many problems are common to all parents.

4. *Cooperation.* The group creates an opportunity for people to learn how to help others. Most of us want to cooperate. Helping others gives us positive feelings. Participating in the give-and-take of a group in a spirit of cooperation, encouragement, and helpfulness can be very gratifying.

The Power and Potential of Problem-Solving Groups

We all want to be effective parents. By becoming a member of a problem-solving group, you can begin to see yourself as your children see you. From this new perspective you can take a fresh look at your parenting. In the group you can get the support and practice you need to turn the *STEP* approach into a practical part of your everyday life.

Notes

1. For more discussion of the concept of perceptual alternatives, see Don Dinkmeyer and Lewis E. Losoncy, *The Encouragement Book: Becoming a Positive Person* (Englewood Cliffs, N.J.: Prentice-Hall, 1980), 181-195.

2. Thomas Gordon, *Parent Effectiveness Training* (New York: Peter H. Wyden, Inc., 1970), 64.

Activity for the Week

After reviewing the information on positive goals in the appendix, identify and encourage your children's positive goals. Typical positive goals include involvement, autonomy, fairness, and withdrawal from conflict.

Family Enrichment Activity

Goal: Learning to see positive possibilities in situations you consider negative.

Choose three situations involving your children that you consider negative. Look for some positive aspects to each situation and plan how you will provide encouragement based on the positive things you see.

Here's an example:

Situation: Your child is associating with children you don't approve of.

Alternative ways of looking at the situation which emphasize the positive:
1. The child is getting to know more people.
2. The child will discover independently that associating with these friends is not in her or his own best interests.

Action: State your opinion about the child's choice of friends in an I-message: "I get really concerned about your hanging around with Bobby and Mike, because they've been in trouble. You might also get in trouble if they do something wrong while you're with them." Using an I-message like this could lead to a productive discussion. If it doesn't, you could decide to trust the child to make his or her own discoveries about these friends. It may turn out that your fears are unfounded.

Situation: _____

_____

_____

Alternative ways of looking at the situation: _____

_____

_____

_____

_____

_____

(continued)

Family Enrichment Activity

Action: _____

_____

_____

Situation: _____

_____

_____

Alternative ways of looking at the situation: _____

_____

_____

_____

_____

_____

Action: _____

_____

_____

Situation: _____

_____

_____

Alternative ways of looking at the situation: _____

_____

_____

_____

_____

_____

Action: _____

_____

_____

Points to Remember

1. Effective parents help children learn to take responsibility for themselves.

2. Parents often hold mistaken beliefs that can block their effectiveness in applying *STEP* principles.

3. You can look at any situation in a variety of ways and choose what meaning you give to events.

4. You can choose to replace unhelpful beliefs with more constructive ones.

5. Humor shifts your attention away from an event's discouraging aspects and puts things in perspective.

6. By working together in problem-solving groups and offering one another support, parents can help each other identify and change mistaken beliefs.

7. Problem-solving groups work best if members
   - treat one another as equals
   - keep a balance between providing and receiving help
   - maintain confidentiality
   - make a commitment to change

8. Acceptance, feedback, universalization, and cooperation are factors that stimulate open, honest, effective interaction in a group.

CHAPTER TWO

Building
Self-Esteem

What Is Self-Esteem?

Self-esteem, or inner confidence and satisfaction with yourself, is the key to effective living. Healthy self-esteem is an unconditional acceptance of yourself. If you have high self-esteem, you accept yourself and your feelings. You have confidence in your opinions. You recognize and use your strengths. You have self-respect.

The way you think and feel about yourself affects the quality of your life. When you feel valuable, lovable, and worthwhile, you are able to meet life's challenges—including the challenges of parenting.

How Do We Learn Self-Esteem?

Our first lessons in self-esteem are learned within the family. Verbally and nonverbally, members of our family constantly send messages to us about our worth. The family atmosphere can either nourish self-esteem or starve it.

Self-esteem is nourished when family members

- show they love and value one another
- allow for individual differences
- appreciate uniqueness
- communicate openly
- look for opportunities to be encouraging
- have a sense of humor
- recognize that it's okay to make mistakes
- find ways to support one another
- share responsibilities

In families where these things happen, members feel good about themselves. They feel valuable and competent. They know they belong.

Here's how one family handled a potentially discouraging situation:

Sayoko, 14, and her sister Chieko, 13, both tried out for the school volleyball team. Chieko made the team, but Sayoko did not. When they came home with the news, their mother, Akiko, seeing that Sayoko was disappointed, said to her, "I'm sorry you didn't make the cut. I know you wanted to be on the team."

Later, Akiko sat down with Sayoko and used reflective listening to give her a chance to talk about her disappointment. She helped Sayoko see some positive options for herself: since she wouldn't be tied up with volleyball practice, she could spend her time after school developing her talent for tennis. Gradually, Sayoko stopped comparing herself to Chieko. Chieko came to watch Sayoko on the tennis court from time to time, and complimented her game.

How Is Self-Esteem Different from Ego-Esteem?

If you have high self-esteem, you are not overly concerned about others' opinions. You know you are valuable just because you are you. But if you have not developed strong self-esteem, you may be using ego-esteem as a substitute. If so, you believe your worth depends on what you have accomplished or what other people think of you. You find yourself constantly trying to please others and wondering, "How am I doing?"

A person with strong self-esteem differs from a person with ego-esteem in the following ways:

Self-esteem	Ego-esteem
Welcomes the unknown	Avoids the unknown; hesitates
Is self-accepting	Is self-rejecting
Is self-affirming	Criticizes self
Is self-controlled	Is controlled by others
Is self-respecting	Doesn't feel respected
Has a strong sense of purpose	Finds little meaning in life
Takes responsibility for own actions	Blames others
Accepts imperfections in self; has a sense of humor and can learn from mistakes	Is overly concerned with mistakes

Your Self-Esteem

In order to encourage your children, you must feel good about yourself. You need your own goals, interests, and friendships to build your self-esteem. If you are entirely wrapped up in your children's lives and goals, your sense of personal worth will be affected too strongly by their successes and failures. So it's important to find and keep an identity that's separate from their behavior and from your parenting role. Remember, your worth doesn't depend on your success as a parent. *You are worthwhile simply because you are human.*

I JUST KNOW THE REASON WE WEREN'T INVITED IS BECAUSE GLORIA DIDN'T MAKE THE CHEERLEADING SQUAD!

Do you let your children's successes or failures affect you too strongly?

Affirming Yourself

To affirm yourself means to value, accept, and appreciate yourself just as you are, with all your imperfections. Self-affirmation requires courage!

You can use positive self-talk to affirm yourself. If you discover you've made the wrong decision, don't think, "That was stupid of me. I am dumb." Instead, affirm yourself: "If I sometimes make the wrong decision, that's okay. I usually make good decisions."

Dorothy Corkille Briggs has suggested that we need to learn how to celebrate ourselves.[1] One way of doing that is to develop and use self-affirmation statements. Here are some examples:

- I make decisions for myself.
- I'm a responsible person.

- I like who I am.
- I can see what's positive in any situation.
- I can see possibilities and alternatives.
- I'm encouraging to others.
- I'm capable and effective in my work.
- I'm worthwhile.

Experiment with saying statements like this to yourself, either out loud or silently. Set aside time to practice them looking in a mirror. Repeat them while you are showering, jogging, driving to work, or simply taking time to relax.

Self-affirmation helps you live with a deep sense of joy about yourself. You appreciate your uniqueness. You realize you don't need to prove yourself or make unrealistic demands on yourself.

Affirming yourself is quite different from bragging or being conceited. Bragging involves comparing yourself to others; it is based on ego-esteem. Self-affirmations identify what you can do without making comparisons. They are a quiet celebration of yourself, a way of being a friend to yourself.

A Self-Affirmation Exercise

This exercise becomes more effective with practice, so don't give up if it doesn't seem to be working at first.

Read through the following instructions before you begin:

Close your eyes and take several deep breaths to relax your body.

Picture yourself sitting in a chair about four feet away.

Think of a quality you want to possess. Now picture yourself having that quality.

Believe that this quality is yours. Claim it for yourself and act as if you already possess it.

Open your eyes.

Have a quiet celebration of yourself.

Self-affirmation helps you increase your own self-esteem. It frees you from the need for external rewards or praise. It enables you to offer others your support and encouragement instead of seeking constant strokes for yourself.

Encouraging Yourself

The way to take charge of your own self-esteem is to provide your own encouragement. To do this, you need to work at being positive about yourself.

In order to encourage yourself, you can

- avoid negative self-talk:

    "I can't get it done."

    "My kids aren't cooperative."

    "It's impossible."

- look for possibilities and solutions, not threats and dangers

- consciously choose how you interpret events and come up with constructive ways of looking at situations

- have a sense of humor and see things in perspective

- make a choice and take responsibility for it, believing that what happens to you is a result of the choices you make

- focus on your strengths and realize that it's not necessary to compare yourself to others

- enjoy your accomplishments

Having the Courage to Be Imperfect

No one can be at his or her best all the time. According to psychiatrist Rudolf Dreikurs, trying to be perfect is likely to leave us feeling dissatisfied and cause us difficulty in our relationships with others.[2]

Do you

- feel comfortable only in the pursuit of perfection?

- have difficulty focusing on the present because your attention is on end results?

- have difficulty enjoying what you are doing because you are afraid of making mistakes?

- tense up out of fear of making a mistake and make more mistakes as a consequence?

If so, then you are probably a perfectionist.

Stop and ask yourself:

- Am I motivated primarily by the desire to help others, to work with them as equals, to be supportive and encouraging? Or,

- Am I most concerned with my status (how others view me)?

- Must I feel more capable than others in order to feel comfortable around them?

If you have a tendency toward perfectionism, remember: Because you are human, mistakes are unavoidable. It's irrational to believe you must be perfect! What you do *after* making a mistake is what's important. Use your mistakes as guides to learning, not indications of worthlessness.

Keeping Expectations Realistic

People with low self-esteem tend to expect too much from themselves and to get discouraged when they fail to live up to their own expectations. Rather than appreciating what they actually accomplish, they may expect more and more of themselves. As parents, they may place high expectations on their children as well. It is not unusual for parents to want their child to accomplish in life what they have not been able to. Take Sam, for example:

Sam did not do well in school himself and barely finished high school. He takes great pride in his son Calvin's good grades and regularly checks on his work. Sam's intentions are good, but his methods have a discouraging effect on Calvin, who feels he can never achieve enough to satisfy his father. Although Calvin does well in school, he still feels inadequate.

Be aware of your expectations. Without realizing it, you could be communicating, "You are worthwhile only when you do what I think is important." Ask yourself these questions:

- Why do I expect this of my child?

- What's in it for me if my child meets this expectation?

- Is this expectation based on something I want for myself or on what would be good for my child?

- Is it realistic to expect my child to be able to do this?

Take time to appreciate yourself. Begin to build your own self-esteem. Then you will find it easier to be realistic in your expectations of others.

Your Child's Self-Esteem

Children usually value themselves only to the extent that they feel valued by the important people in their lives—parents, siblings, relatives, teachers, friends. The messages they get from you need to be encouraging.

Self-Esteem and the Child's Development

Self-esteem comes from positive experiences, beginning in infancy. As your children develop, their abilities will increase. If you expect them to be able to do things beyond their capacity, or if you expect too little from them, they will be discouraged. Realistic expectations are encouraging.

Children reach milestones when they are developmentally ready: sitting up, walking, using the toilet. But the milestones in a child's maturing process can't always be recognized easily. For example, we may be reluctant to see that our teenagers are ready to make their own decisions.

Keep in mind that self-confidence means being able to say, "I can do it myself." Allow your children to have that experience as early and as often as possible. As soon as they are able, let them bathe themselves, dress themselves, prepare their own snacks. *Never do for your children what they can do for themselves.*[3]

If you expect your children to be able to do things beyond their capacity, or if you expect too little of them, they will be discouraged.

Infancy. It's important for infants to develop trust. When your baby cries and you respond, the baby learns

- to trust you

- to trust that communicating his or her needs will get results

- to trust that the world is a safe place to be[4]

If you don't respond, your baby may learn, on a feeling level, "My needs aren't important." Holding, cuddling, talking, and rocking are ways parents meet the infant's needs for attention and touch. The child's feeling "I have the right to be" comes from these early experiences of learning to trust.

But if you anticipate your baby's needs before they are expressed, the baby may not learn to make the important connection between expression and response. And if a baby gets unnecessary, fussy attention the instant she makes a sound, she may learn to demand constant attention. Be responsive, but remember that all children must learn eventually that they're not the center of the universe.

The period of exploration. Toddlers learn about the environment by looking, touching, and putting things in their mouths. They also experiment with self-expression, making sounds and faces to see what response they get. If we give them appreciative responses and encourage them to explore, their self-esteem will grow.

Provide a safe environment, but don't put too many restrictions on your child's exploration. Too many "no-no's" are discouraging. And to stop exploring is to stop learning. Of course, childproof your home as much as possible so exploration will be safe. When restrictions are necessary, it helps to give choices: "You can squeeze your ball or your teddy bear, but not the puppy."

Preschool and early primary years. After the period of exploration, children begin to develop independence—to see themselves as separate from their parents. Encouraging this independence fosters their self-esteem.

During this period, children establish their identity as they learn about their world. They learn how they are expected to act. They learn to separate fantasy from reality.

You help your children form their identities, not only by encouraging imagination and helping them acquire information, but by setting limits and giving them feedback. Remember their budding self-esteem and take care not to criticize or ridicule them.[5] Suppose your five-year-old son is displaying poor table manners by stuffing squash into his mouth with his fingers. You may feel like saying, "Stop eating like a pig!" Instead, calmly remind him, "We eat squash with our forks."

Elementary school years. During this time, children discover their own way of doing things. They develop strong likes and dislikes. You can continue to nourish their self-esteem by giving them more choices and accepting their preferences whenever possible. Natural and logical consequences will allow them to learn cause and effect as they test their limits. Encourage them to take reasonable risks. Help them begin to make the connection between accepting responsibility and developing independence.

Adolescence. In order to become independent adults, teens must increasingly separate themselves from the family. Their methods may not be graceful. They may challenge family values and develop friendships unacceptable to you. You can help them to become more independent in a positive way by using encouragement and natural and logical consequences.

As teenagers attempt
to separate themselves from the family,
their methods may not be graceful.

Building Your Child's Self-Esteem

Here are effective ways for you to build your child's self-esteem at any age:

- Give feedback that makes a clear distinction between the behavior and the person. Let your actions communicate "I don't like what you are doing, but I still love you."

- Encourage independence: "I know you can solve that by yourself."

- Give responsibility and expect cooperation: "I'll take care of the laundry, if you'll put your dirty clothes in the hamper."

- Accept mistakes. In schoolwork, instead of focusing on errors, encourage the child: "Look how many answers you got right!" You may want to show that you accept mistakes by not commenting on them at all.

- Encourage your child to see the humorous side of events: "I like your sense of humor." Show you can laugh at yourself. Take care never to appear to be laughing at your child.

- Encourage self-appreciation: "You sound pleased with your work."

- Accept and value the child's uniqueness: "You're very imaginative."

- Be positive:

  "I'll bet we can figure out a solution. What ideas do you have?"

  "I know you're sad to move away from this neighborhood, but our new house will be close to the park."

Seeing What's Positive

There are many experiences in your child's life over which you have little or no control. Some are potentially discouraging, both to your child and to you. But, as discussed in Chapter One, we choose how we see and interpret events. By identifying and expressing a positive viewpoint, you show your children a powerful tool for building self-esteem.

In theory, looking for what's positive should take the same amount of effort as noticing the negative. But sometimes it can seem more difficult—most of us have more practice noticing what's wrong. Still, looking for the positive is a skill that can really pay off. When you feel disappointed or discouraged, take time to think of an encouraging way of looking at the situation. Communicate this view to your children. You will probably begin to notice positive changes in them.

Suppose your child earns a low grade on a social studies paper. If you point out the mistakes in the paper, you will probably only add to the discouraging effect of the low grade. You can be encouraging by talking about what the child did well: difficult words spelled correctly, facts presented accurately, the effort you know went into it.

Or suppose your child is in a gymnastics event and loses by one point. Saying "You lost your big chance" is discouraging. If you can point out something positive about the performance without being insincere, that would probably be more helpful: "You're really improving. I really liked the way you landed on the first flip."

Self-Esteem and Academic Achievement

High self-esteem is especially important for success in school. In fact, research indicates that a positive self-concept is more important to academic success than a high I.Q. score.[6] Children who have learned self-confidence and self-acceptance at home are more likely to do well in school. You can build your children's self-esteem by letting them take responsibility for their own academic work.

Self-Esteem When the Family Structure Changes

Although new parents hope and intend to preserve their family intact, parenting is increasingly being done in single parent families or stepfamilies. Changes in family structure mean that the adults and the children involved must redefine their roles and relationships. All family members face this task, whether they wanted the change or not. Self-esteem can be affected.

Divorce and Self-Esteem

Divorce creates special challenges for both parents and children. When a marriage ends—even if the separation or divorce may eventually improve everyone's situation—many factors can contribute to a temporary drop in parents' and children's self-esteem.

Parents may blame and find fault with each other. There may be a tug-of-war over children as well as possessions. A divorcing parent may feel angry with his or her spouse and want the children to take sides, undermining their relationship with the other parent.

Parents may be so discouraged by their own problems that they have little time and energy for the children. If their own self-esteem is low, parents may find it difficult to help their children feel secure and to model self-confidence for them.

In this discouraging environment, children may not feel very good about themselves. They may feel abandoned and even fear they caused the divorce. Their behavior may change as they attempt to deal with their feelings. Quiet, studious children may skip school, refuse to study, bring home poor grades, and begin to act out. Happy, outgoing children may become withdrawn and refuse to interact with friends or be involved in activities. Behavior changes of this kind may be a response to loss.

Parents and children urgently need their own support systems at this time. Parents can take steps to get help for themselves from a friend or relative, a counselor, a member of the clergy, or a support group, such as Parents Without Partners. They can also arrange for their children to get help—from friends, relatives, professionals, or a group like Big Brothers or Big Sisters.

Parents need high self-esteem to meet the challenges associated with separation and divorce. It may help to remind yourself that the self-esteem you had before the divorce can be regained or even improved upon. Life can still be tackled with enthusiasm and courage. Parents can

- focus on their strengths
- practice self-encouragement
- use affirming statements that relate to the challenges they are experiencing:

  "I'm my own person."

  "I can help my children through this experience."

  "I can go on with my life."
- visualize themselves meeting their goals.[7]

Divorce is never easy, but these skills can help parents get through it with their self-esteem intact.

Self-Esteem in the Stepfamily

New stepparents often have unrealistic expectations about the stepparenting relationship. They may expect a good relationship with their stepchildren from the beginning. But

New stepparents often have
unrealistic expectations about
the stepparenting relationship.

the children may not at first see any benefits from the
remarriage. They may be struggling with feelings of
betrayal, resentment, resistance to change.

Newly married stepparents need to plan time for activities
that strengthen their own self-esteem, particularly since
they will be modeling self-esteem for the children. Here are
guidelines for an activity many couples have found helpful:

*1. Sit down facing each other in a quiet, private place. You
may want to hold hands.*

*2. Tell your partner, "The most positive thing that happened
today was . . ." Then go on to say, "Something I appreciated
about you today was . . ." Take three to five minutes.*

*3. Ask your partner to feed back the ideas, beliefs, feelings,
or values she or he has heard.*

4. While your partner takes three to five minutes to complete those same sentences, listen attentively and do not interrupt. Maintain eye contact.

5. Feed back to your partner what you have heard.

Additional topics that can be used in the same format are

- "The most enjoyable thing I did this week was . . ."
- "Something I enjoy about you is . . ."
- "Something I'm looking forward to doing with you is . . ."[8]

Another way stepparents can refuel to meet the challenges they face is by regularly setting aside time for self-encouragement and self-affirmation.

Bringing two families together is a big challenge for anyone. Conflicts related to the children are common and can affect the marriage relationship. It takes time to start to feel like a real family. Be realistic in your expectations.

Communication and decision-making skills are especially helpful in stepfamilies. Family meetings provide an opportunity to make plans cooperatively. They give children a voice in the new family structure and a sense that their opinion is valued.

Taking Charge of Your Self-Esteem

No matter what your family structure, self-esteem can energize you to move positively through the day. You can create an atmosphere in your home that nurtures everyone's self-esteem.

Even in the midst of great change in your life you can maintain your own self-esteem and model self-esteem for your children. When you are self-encouraged, you are able to make choices and take responsibility for those choices.

Trust your evaluation of the world. Instead of depending on others' appraisals of you, create your own positive self-appraisal. Don't spend your time wondering what people will think or worrying about trying to "look good."

Become a self-affirming person. Celebrate yourself as you are.

Notes

1. Dorothy Corkille Briggs, *Celebrate Yourself* (Garden City, N.Y.: Doubleday and Co., 1977).

2. Janet Terner and W. L. Pew, *The Courage to Be Imperfect* (New York: Hawthorn, 1978).

3. Rudolf Dreikurs and Vickie Soltz, *Children: The Challenge* (New York: Hawthorn, 1964), 193.

4. Jean Illsley Clarke, *Self-Esteem: A Family Affair* (Minneapolis: Winston Press, 1978), 44.

5. Clarke, 136-37.

6. William Wattenberg and C. Clifford, "Relationship of Self-Concepts to Beginning Achievement in Reading," *Child Development* 35 (1964): 461-67.

7. Don Dinkmeyer, *Self-Encouragement and Self-Hypnosis: A Route to Self-Mastery,* audiocassette (Coral Springs, Fla.: CMTI Press, 1985).

8. Don Dinkmeyer and Jon Carlson, *Time for a Better Marriage* (Circle Pines, Minn.: American Guidance Service, 1984), 27.

Activity for the Week

Make a list of self-affirmations and practice reading them aloud at least once a day. For example: "I like who I am," "I'm capable and effective."

Family Enrichment Activity

Everyone in your family has a specific level of self-esteem that can be influenced.

1. List each member of your family below, including yourself and your spouse if you are married.

2. Rate each person's level of self-esteem on a scale of 1 (low self-esteem) to 5 (high self-esteem).

3. Who do you think has the lowest self-esteem? How might that person be helped by the others? As you begin to explore, you may find ways for even the most discouraged family members to help encourage others.

Name: _____

Level of self-esteem: _____

Ways to encourage: _____

_____

_____

Name: _____

Level of self-esteem: _____

Ways to encourage: _____

_____

_____

Name: _____

Level of self-esteem: _____

Ways to encourage: _____

_____

_____

Family Enrichment Activity

Name: _____

Level of self-esteem: _____

Ways to encourage: _____

_____

_____

Name: _____

Level of self-esteem: _____

Ways to encourage: _____

_____

_____

Name: _____

Level of self-esteem: _____

Ways to encourage: _____

_____

_____

4. Implement your plans for encouragement this week.

Points to Remember

1. Self-esteem is the key to effective living.

2. Self-esteem comes from within.

3. Ego-esteem is based on accomplishments and the opinions of others.

4. You are worthwhile because you are you. You do not have to earn your worth by being an effective parent.

5. Raising your self-esteem as a parent strengthens the self-esteem of the entire family.

6. Self-affirmation increases your self-esteem.

7. A self-encouraging person is one who sees possibilities and solutions, not threats and dangers.

8. A sense of humor assists in building self-esteem.

9. Perfectionism destroys self-esteem.

10. The courage to be imperfect helps you develop self-esteem. You can model this courage for your children.

11. Overprotection and criticism hinder the development of a child's self-esteem.

12. You can help your children build self-esteem by encouraging them and by emphasizing the positive.

13. Children who feel good about themselves are more likely to do well in school.

14. Keeping a high level of self-esteem will help you cope with changes in family structure.

CHAPTER THREE

How Lifestyle Beliefs Affect Your Parenting

Developing an Approach to Life

Now that you've had some practice identifying the mistaken beliefs that influence parents' behavior, perhaps you are wondering, "Where do these beliefs come from?" According to Adler, beliefs about what we must do in order to belong begin to develop early in life, even before we learn to talk.[1]

As children, we are born into a unique, ongoing situation. It's as though we find ourselves in the middle of the second act of a play, says psychologist Robert L. Powers, and we have to "ad lib" our way into the action. We size up the situation and find a role for ourselves in the play by asking, " 'What's going on here? What kind of world is this? What kind of person am I? What must I do, and what must I become in order to get in on things?' " Then we act out the answers we've decided on. Through trial and error we develop a role for ourselves, and usually we continue to act out that role as adults. We also choose a goal:

- to be the star, with everyone else in a supporting role

or,

- to be a member of the cast who takes the attitude that "the show must go on."[2]

In this way we develop a characteristic approach to life—what Adler called a *lifestyle.* Our lifestyle is reflected in our beliefs, values, goals, and priorities, and in the meaning we give to our experience.

We develop a role for ourselves,
and usually we continue
to act out that role as adults.

What Influences
Lifestyle Development?

There are five major influences on lifestyle:

1. *heredity*—the child's inherited physical characteristics

2. *family atmosphere and values*—the relationship climate in the home (strict or relaxed, permissive or democratic, orderly or chaotic, discouraging or encouraging) and parents' values (such as those concerning education, money, hard work, religion, success, achievement)

3. the child's *role models*—parents, teachers, other significant adults

4. *methods of training* parents use

5. the child's psychological position in the *family constellation,* often based on birth order. (See the appendix for a chart showing some typical characteristics of family constellation positions.)*

Why Are Lifestyle Beliefs Mistaken?

We choose our lifestyle beliefs early, between the ages of four and six, a time when we often feel uncertain of ourselves and inferior to the adults around us. As a result, we are likely to choose lifestyle beliefs based on our need to overcome these negative feelings.[3] These beliefs express the conviction that we must *do* something in order to belong. Since that's a mistaken idea—we belong just because we're part of the human family—all lifestyle beliefs are based on a faulty premise.

As young children, we are keen observers, but we don't always interpret what we see correctly. By generalizing on the basis of very limited experience, we come to mistaken conclusions. And we tend to carry those conclusions into adulthood.

For example, if we're competing with a brother or sister, we may decide, "I must be the best." If our parents break promises to us, we may conclude, "You can't trust anybody." A boy abused by his mother may decide, "Stay away from Mother; she's dangerous." This may be a good decision in regard to his mother. But unfortunately, he may generalize and go on to conclude, "All women are dangerous."

How Does Lifestyle Affect Relationships?

Our lifestyle beliefs can either help or hurt us in our efforts to meet life's challenges. Believing "I must be the best" can spur us to accomplish great things. But it can also interfere

---

*There is a detailed discussion of these five influences on pages 25-31 of *The Parent's Guide* from *STEP/Teen*.

with developing good relationships. Beliefs like "You can't trust anybody" or "All women are dangerous" will also hamper relationships and make it difficult to get close to others.

Can Lifestyles Change?

Even though we live by our beliefs about how to belong, we are often not aware of them. As long as we don't examine our beliefs, they aren't likely to change. People tend to keep the same beliefs throughout life, even mistaken ones.

However, experience can change our beliefs. Traumatic experiences may influence people to adopt less trusting beliefs or to re-examine the meaning of life. Positive experiences that can help people become aware of their beliefs and change them are

- successful therapy
- religious conversion
- personal growth that increases self-esteem

Experiences like these can lead us to realize that we have a place in life and are worthwhile just because we're human, neither better nor worse than other people. Then we can develop our capacity for cooperation.

The Personality Priorities

Our decisions about what is important in life—our priorities—are reflected in our relationships with others. By asking ourselves what we value in relationships, we can find clues to our lifestyle beliefs. Although no two lifestyles are exactly alike, people with the same priorities usually have a number of lifestyle beliefs in common. Most lifestyle beliefs reflect one of these four priorities:

- superiority
- control
- pleasing
- comfort [4]

These are known as the personality priorities. Pursuing them helps us achieve a sense of belonging.

To the extent that we accept ourselves and realize that we don't actually have to do anything special to belong, we will also have a fifth priority:

- social interest

People with this priority want to further society's interests. To that end, they work cooperatively with others rather than in competition with them. They participate in the give-and-take of life. People with a high degree of social interest are contributors. They care about people and show compassion for them.

Someone who had fully achieved the social interest priority would use the other four priorities in a positive way, choosing priorities on the basis of what fitted a particular situation—the ideal way to behave. Though none of us is perfect, we can each aim toward this ideal and strive to grow as people and as parents.

On some level, we decide which priorities are most important to us. But most of us don't consciously choose the priority that best fits a given situation. Instead, our mistaken beliefs lead us to value certain priorities whether they're appropriate to the circumstances we find ourselves in or not. We get attached to certain priorities and lose our flexibility. Consider Jessie:

Jessie values her physical comfort and likes to feel she's in control. She tries to arrange her home and her family life so she can count on things running smoothly. But recently her job has begun to require a lot of overtime. Because she is never sure what time she will get home, she is very anxious and uncomfortable. She likes to relax right after work before making dinner, but now she feels there is no time for that. Because of her need to control, she feels no one else is capable of making dinner—she has to plunge in and start cooking as soon as she walks in the door. Due to her anxiety, her resentment at being deprived of her comfort, and her struggle to keep things in order, she is irritable. When the kids are tired and cranky, she finds herself getting into conflicts with them.

Jessie is suffering from lack of flexibility. Her interest in control and her attachment to comfort are keeping her from being able to "roll with the punches."

The beliefs that underlie the personality priorities can be expressed in a variety of ways, some positive, some negative. For example, if we believe we must be superior, we may express this either by working hard at a task, or by avoiding the task because we see no chance of being best at it. The child who wants to be "the best" may grow up to be a successful scientist—or a successful criminal. Most people act out their lifestyle beliefs in both positive and negative ways. Courage, self-esteem, and social interest help us to act out our beliefs positively.

Let's look further at the negative and positive sides of the four personality priorities and see how each priority affects relationships, especially parent-child relationships. *As you read, you may recognize your negative side, but it will be helpful to focus on your assets. Keep in mind that no priority is better or worse than the others. And remember, nobody is completely summed up by one priority.*

Superiority

People who value superiority may believe they must be better than others in some way. Without superiority, they feel, life is meaningless. They often believe they have to be competent and useful in order to prove they are worthwhile. They may doubt themselves and crave the reassurance of being recognized as "the best."

Some lifestyle beliefs commonly held by superiority seekers are

- I must be the best.
- I must be perfect.
- I know what's best.
- I am the smartest.
- I am special and should get special treatment.

It's quite a burden to carry around beliefs like these! People who have superiority as their goal may feel overburdened, short of time, uncertain of their standing with others, guilty. They fear failure and defeat. They may have poor relationships with others—an attitude of superiority can turn people off or leave them feeling inadequate.

People who place a high value
on superiority crave the reassurance
of being recognized as "the best."

Pressure to live up to the standards of a perfectionist parent can leave children feeling, "Nothing I do is ever right," or "Nothing I do is good enough." Children who feel this way may become superiority-seekers or perfectionists themselves, or they may get discouraged and give up.

Parents who value superiority are prone to pity their children, to overprotect them, and to take over their responsibilities. The children may then feel sorry for themselves and always expect others to help them.

Developing the Positive Side of Superiority

People who seek superiority can have many worthy qualities, based on their respect for excellence—responsibility, ambition, courage, perceptiveness. They are often creative and knowledgeable as parents. They can use their assets to help children discover their own resources and strengths. Superiority-seekers are also likely to be idealistic. They can help their children develop a positive outlook on life and can encourage them to work to improve society.

If you suspect yourself of inclining toward superiority, you can choose to develop these assets. You can also make a conscious effort to avoid doing anything that would invite your children to feel inferior. Give your children responsibility, expect them to contribute, let them own their own problems. Pay particular attention to nourishing their self-esteem: believe in them, respect them, appreciate them.

Appreciate yourself too. Be more self-accepting. If you're troubled by feelings of guilt about not living up to your standards, you may have set them too high. If you find you're sacrificing yourself to your family, take time for yourself. Expect other family members to do their share.

Control

People who place a high value on controlling others can use a variety of means to do so—logic, temper, charm, tears ("water power"), dependent behavior (to make others take care of them), stubbornness, resistance, and avoiding feelings (to keep people at a distance). They may fear that unless they're in control, others will humiliate them. Controllers want to avoid embarrassment. They fear the unexpected, and they're afraid of being wrong. They want to create an orderly world, because this helps them feel in control. They strongly resist being controlled themselves. They want to know everything, have absolute power, and be perfect; only then can they feel certain of having a place.

Some beliefs commonly held by people who have this priority are

- I must be in control of myself.
- I must be in control of others.
- I must have my own way.
- I must be the boss.
- I must not get too close to people.
- People should take care of my needs.
- I must protect others.

People who place a high value on self-control have difficulty acknowledging their feelings. This may communicate to their children that it's not okay to feel. It's also one of the reasons some controllers have trouble making friends and getting close to people. Getting close would mean taking the lid off their feelings and letting down the barriers that help them feel in control. Getting close would leave them feeling vulnerable.

Also, most people don't want to be controlled and choose not to get close to someone who wants to control them. So controllers may feel lonely and distant from people. Their lives may lack creativity and spontaneity. They put a lot of effort into trying to make life predictable. When the unpredictable occurs, they may lack the flexibility to deal with it effectively.

Parents who place a high value
on controlling their children can use
a variety of means to do so.

Children usually don't like to be controlled. So parents who believe they must control often find themselves in power contests with their children. The anger these parents generate by trying to maintain control, win conflicts, or prove they are right just fuels the child's own desire for power. Children who don't resist the controlling parent may become overly dependent.

Developing the Positive Side of Control

Many assets are related to having control as a high priority. People who value control may be well-organized and like structure. They define things clearly and tend to be good planners. They often make good leaders. They are usually self-starters, industrious and persistent. They model self-sufficiency for their children.

The orderly world created by parents who value control can offer the structure and stability children need. The emotional restraint of these parents may work to their advantage in dealing with their children's misbehavior.

Parents with this priority need to focus on controlling the situation, not the child. They can do this by working at giving choices within the guidelines they provide. They can involve their older children in deciding what a situation requires and in setting limits and consequences.

Pleasing

People who have pleasing as their priority believe they must have approval from others and will do almost anything to get it. They can't bear rejection—it means they have failed to please. They commonly hold lifestyle beliefs such as these:

- I must please others.

- I must be liked by everyone all the time.

- I must gain everyone's approval for everything I do.

- I must avoid rejection.

- Others should appreciate what I do for them.

Pleasers pay a high price for their priority. The attempt to please everyone divides their energies and restricts their personal growth. Since they often let others take advantage of them, they have difficulty respecting themselves and others. They also have difficulty winning respect. The people they try to please may actually feel pleased at first. But eventually they may feel disgusted or aggravated by the pleaser's constant attempts to win approval.

Parents who place a high value on pleasing will do almost anything to please their children—whether or not it's in the child's best interests. They may spoil their children or take over their responsibilities. They may try to buy their children's love and approval with gifts and favors. This puts pressure on the children. Children whose parents are focused on pleasing them may grow up to be selfish.

Parents who place a high value
on pleasing will do almost anything
to please their children.

Developing the Positive Side of Pleasing

On the positive side, pleasers are people concerned with others. They tend to be friendly, perceptive, sensitive, and understanding. They are usually generous, affectionate, and kind, and they make friends easily. They are good at perceiving how their children feel and what they want. They are sensitive to their children's concerns. These parents have fewer conflicts with their children, since they are usually diplomatic and avoid confrontation.

Parents with a priority of pleasing need to be firm as well as kind when they encounter a situation requiring consequences. They have to be careful not to let their children take advantage of their generosity. They need to take care of themselves and not spend all their time trying to satisfy others.

Comfort

People who put their own comfort first believe they must avoid pain, stress, and responsibility. They don't want others to expect things from them; they don't want to feel cornered. Some lifestyle beliefs commonly held by comfort seekers are

- I must avoid pain, whether physical or emotional.

- I must avoid conflict and stress.

- I must avoid responsibility.

- People should not expect anything from me.

- I am inadequate.

- Life should be easy.

- I should get what I want when I want it.

People who always put comfort first often don't make full use of their talents. So they're not as productive as they could be. Because they're usually looking out for their own comfort, others are likely to feel annoyed or bored with them.

Most people like a certain degree of comfort—physical and psychological. But parents who place a high value on their own comfort and never put their children's wishes first invite resentment and revenge. For example, suppose your daughter wants you to take her to a ball game. Instead of welcoming the opportunity for an outing with her, you want to avoid the drive and the crowds. For her, the excitement of being there is important. If she feels that you never consider what she wants, she may decide to get even with you.

Some comfort seekers try to make certain their children are comfortable too. But assuming this responsibility for children can deny them the opportunity to grow. Letting your children take care of their own comfort helps them learn responsibility.

Parents who place a high value
on their own comfort invite revenge.

Developing the Positive Side of Comfort

Comfort seekers tend to be easygoing and undemanding
parents. Like pleasers, they want to keep the peace and
avoid conflicts. For this reason, they are usually good at letting children work out their own problems. Their undemanding style doesn't usually provoke rebellion in their
children.

Raising Cooperative Children

In reading about the personality priorities, you have probably considered which descriptions best fit you. You may
also have asked yourself which best fit your children. If they
are six or older, their personality priorities have probably
been established. However, when you respond to their mis-

behavior, it is more practical and effective for you to concentrate on their goals of misbehavior. These goals change depending on how the child sees the immediate situation— and it is the immediate situation you must deal with. In considering our children's personality priorities, we need mainly to concern ourselves with whether they are developing a priority of social interest by learning cooperation.

At various times in our relationships with our children, we've all felt superior to them, desperate to control them, anxious to please them, or tempted to ignore them while putting our own comfort first. But we don't want them to feel that

- nothing they ever do is good enough

- they must constantly struggle for power

- they were born to get their own way rather than to cooperate

- they have to hurt us to get back at us for ignoring them

We want to develop cooperation in the family. By making an effort to develop the positive side of our personality priorities and by considering others' interests as well as our own, we can model cooperation for our children and improve our relationships.

We want our children to learn to take care of themselves, to be responsible, to make good decisions, and to be able to get along well with others. We want them to become cooperative, contributing members of society. This is most likely to happen if we give them the chance to experience cooperation firsthand by treating them as coworkers in a democratic family.

We can also help our children move toward cooperation by giving them lots of encouragement and nourishing their self-esteem. The trust required for true cooperation is first learned within the family. The encouragement we provide allows trust to flourish.

Achieving Flexibility for Ourselves

Thinking about the negative aspects of the personality priorities can be discouraging. Society has trained us well to ask ourselves, "What am I doing wrong?" If you see the negative side of the personality priorities in yourself, remember that as a child you had what seemed like good reasons for adopting superiority, control, pleasing, or comfort as a strategy for belonging. Have some compassion for yourself and for others who live under the tyranny of beliefs like "I must be perfect."

It can be useful to recognize your mistaken beliefs and to work on changing them. The next chapter will offer some strategies for choosing more constructive beliefs. It can also be helpful to become aware of what you are seeking to avoid—feeling useless, humiliated, rejected, cornered. It can be illuminating to realize why others may have been reacting negatively to your behavior.

But recognizing your assets is even more important. We all have some measure of courage, ambition, desire to do things well, organization, leadership, friendliness, sensitivity, empathy, the ability to be relaxed in our relationship with others. We all would like to have relationships based on loving cooperation. We can all choose to work toward that goal.

You can learn to emphasize the side of your priorities that will strengthen your relationships with others—you can learn to lead rather than to overpower, for example. You can learn to choose a positive way to use a priority to fit a particular situation. Flexibility in using your priorities will make you a more effective parent.

Notes

1. Heinz L. and Rowena R. Ansbacher, eds., *The Individual Psychology of Alfred Adler* (New York: Harper and Row, 1956), 180-188.

2. Robert L. Powers, "Myth and Memory," in *Alfred Adler: His Influence on Psychology Today,* ed. Harold H. Mosak (Park Ridge, N.J.: Noyes Press, 1973), 275.

3.Rudolf Dreikurs, "The Private Logic," in *Alfred Adler: His Influence on Psychology Today,* ed. Harold H. Mosak (Park Ridge, N.J.: Noyes Press, 1973), 22-23.

4. Nira Kefir and Raymond Corsini, "Dispositional Sets: A Contribution to Typology," *Journal of Individual Psychology* 30 (November 1974): 163-78.

Activity for the Week

Undertake some project that involves working together as a family—doing yard work, cleaning out the attic, painting a room, preparing a meal. Use the opportunity for give-and-take this project provides to develop the social interest priority in family members. Practice cooperation.

Family Enrichment Activity

Part 1. Self-Evaluation Inventory

The following statements are grouped according to the personality priority they are believed to reflect. Read them and indicate how true each statement is for you by using the following scale:

Never	Seldom	Sometimes	Often	Always
1	2	3	4	5

Group A

_____ I find I can do most tasks better than other people.
_____ I make sure the tasks I do involve significant contributions.
_____ I work hard, accomplishing much more than most people.
_____ I strive to be the best in what I choose to do.

Group B

_____ I am busy; I can handle two or more projects at a time.
_____ I am determined to have my plans carried out.
_____ I am a self-starter.
_____ I work to make sure things are done right.

Group C

_____ I thrive on praise from others.
_____ I must gain approval from people who are important to me.
_____ I am sensitive to others' opinions of me.
_____ I have difficulty saying no.

Group D

_____ I have difficulty getting things done.
_____ I dislike responsibility.
_____ I have difficulty handling stress.
_____ I dislike it when people put expectations on me.

Now rate yourself by using the scoring key at the end of this Family Enrichment Activity.

Then ask yourself whether you believe your highest scores accurately reflect the priorities you value most. If not, why not? _____

_____

_____

Family Enrichment Activity

Part 2. Applying the Priorities to Your Parenting

Answer the following questions:

1. Which of the personality priorities do you think you value most: superiority, control, pleasing, or comfort? _____

2. Describe a situation in which you remember using the positive side of your priority with your children. _____

_____

_____

_____

_____

What were the results for the children? _____

_____

_____

_____

3. Describe a situation in which you used a negative aspect of your priority with your children. _____

_____

_____

_____

_____

How did the children react? _____

_____

_____

_____

(continued)

Family Enrichment Activity

4. What are some things you can do this week to use the positive side of your priority with your children? _____

_____

_____

_____

_____

_____

5. What signs of the social interest priority do you see in yourself?

_____

_____

_____

_____

In your children? _____

_____

_____

_____

_____

6. How can you consciously expand your social interest? _____

_____

_____

_____

_____

The social interest of your children? _____

_____

_____

_____

_____

_____

Family Enrichment Activity

Scoring Key

Add up your self-rating for the four items in each group to get a total score for the group.

	Your total score	Average score*	Priority the items are believed to reflect
Group A	_____	14.5	Superiority
Group B	_____	16.1	Control
Group C	_____	13.6	Pleasing
Group D	_____	10.4	Comfort

*These were the mean scores of a sample of 100 people who completed the inventory when it was field tested.

Points to Remember

1. Lifestyle is the characteristic approach to life we develop when we are young by observing our world and interpreting our experience.

2. The five major influences on lifestyle development are heredity, family atmosphere and values, role models, methods of training, and family constellation.

3. Lifestyle beliefs are based on a mistaken premise: that we are worthless and insignificant unless we behave in a certain way.

4. As we become aware of our beliefs, we can reconsider them and make changes if we see they aren't helping us.

5. The personality priorities are superiority, control, pleasing, and comfort.

6. The social interest priority involves cooperating with others in order to further society's interests.

7. The personality priorities can be acted out in both positive and negative ways.

8. Parents who value superiority must be careful not to let their high standards discourage their children.

9. Parents who value control can avoid power struggles by controlling the situation, not the child.

Points to Remember

10. Parents who value pleasing need to be firm as well as kind.

11. Parents who value comfort need to make an effort to accommodate their children's wishes occasionally.

12. When making decisions about how to deal with children, considering their goals of misbehavior is more effective than looking for their personality priorities.

13. Using your priorities more flexibly will make you a more effective parent.

CHAPTER FOUR

Stress:
Coping with Changes
and Challenges

Stress and the Family

Change of any kind can be stressful. So can everyday annoyances and frustrations. We are accustomed to think of events such as death, divorce, major illness, or loss of a job as stressful. But people may also experience stress when they go through positive changes—the birth of a baby, remarriage, a new job. Potentially stressful situations are a part of life for every family.

Stress, whether stimulated by events in or outside the home, can affect your relationships with other family members and your parenting. This chapter will show you how to use skills you already have to deal effectively with stress— encouraging and appreciating yourself, accepting your feelings, having the courage to be imperfect, remembering that you can choose how you see events. It will also make you aware of the effect some common family stresses can have on your children and will suggest ways you can help. Finally, the chapter will offer some methods of relaxation you and your children can use to reduce stress.

What Is Stress?

Stress is the physical and emotional response we experience when we view an event as upsetting. Potentially stressful situations are always with us. Even everyday events such as a hurried morning routine can be experienced as stressful. But events alone do not create stress. Our perceptions and beliefs are the culprits.

For example, some people love to argue; they rise to the challenge. Arguments aren't stressful for them. But for people who are uncomfortable with conflict, arguments may be very stressful. *Stress is directly related to the meaning we give to a situation.*

If we recognize that we can choose how we see events, we will be far less likely to experience a situation as stressful. We can also learn to control and alter the physical and emotional responses involved in a stress reaction. We can learn to relax and to choose less upsetting ways of thinking about our experience.

How We Create Stress

Psychologists Albert Ellis and Robert A. Harper provide a useful model for understanding how we think ourselves into strong upset feelings and how we can think ourselves out of them. They explain their model in terms of *A, B, C.*

- *A* stands for the *activating* event—something you find very upsetting.

- *B* represents your *belief* about *A,* the activating event.

- *C* stands for the emotional *consequence* of your belief about the activating event.[1]

Here is an example. Let's assume you've taken a *STEP* course and are getting along well with your children. But one day you slip and yell at them. You say to yourself, "How awful! I made a stupid mistake yelling at the kids. I can't stand making mistakes. I should not make mistakes. I'm really a bad parent!" This kind of thinking is stressful. When you tell yourself these things, the emotional consequence is anger and discouragement.

How did you get yourself into this state? You might conclude you are experiencing these emotions because you made a mistake with the children. In other words, your yelling—*A,* the activating event—caused *C,* the emotional consequence. But is that true? Some parents yell at their children and don't seem to get at all upset with themselves. In fact, *A* did not cause *C.* What caused *C* was your thinking at point *B*—your belief about the event.

Your belief that you should not make mistakes, according to Ellis and Harper, is irrational. Where is the law that says you should not make mistakes? People make mistakes all the time! Berating yourself isn't going to change anything. Also, who says you "can't stand making mistakes"? It isn't so awful to make a mistake! And making one mistake doesn't make you a "bad parent." Most of the time, you get along very well with your children.

An irrational belief has four parts: catastrophizing, "can't-stand-it-itis,"[2] commanding, and condemning. The above example can be used to illustrate.

Catastrophizing: "How awful! I made a stupid mistake."

"Can't-stand-it-itis": "I can't stand making mistakes."

Commanding: "I should not make mistakes."

Condemning: "I'm really a bad parent!"

The root of the irrational belief is the command—the *should* or *must.* If you didn't command yourself to be or to behave a certain way, you wouldn't engage in catastrophizing, condemning, and "can't-stand-it-itis."

Commands—The Tyranny of *Must* and *Should*

Commands are absolute: they use *should, must, have to, always, never.* Absolute thinking blocks the flexibility and creativity necessary for problem solving; it also leaves us stuck with our strong upset feelings.

It's okay to be aware of your preferences. But if you try to command reality to be a certain way, you are inviting discouragement. Reality can't be changed just by commanding it. That isn't the way life operates. What you wish reality to be is just that—a wish. When you define your wishes as needs, you set yourself up for stress when you don't get what you "need."

Because the mistaken lifestyle beliefs associated with the personality priorities are commands, they are a major source of stress. We can't always be in control, always be

Irrational beliefs can lead you
to exaggerate a situation.

the best, or always please everyone. Eternal comfort is no more attainable than eternal youth.

Understanding your personality priority will make it easier to catch yourself in irrational beliefs and will suggest what direction to take to make your beliefs more realistic. We can lead more satisfying lives with less stress when we have realistic beliefs about life and can accept our own limitations and imperfections.

Choosing More Realistic Beliefs

You can reduce your anxiety and level of stress by changing your irrational beliefs to rational ones. To the *A, B, C* of irrational beliefs, you can add a *D* and *dispute* irrational beliefs by changing your language and your thinking.[3]

Let's return to the example of yelling at your children. This time let's focus on reducing stress by choosing different beliefs about the event. Suppose you choose to say, "I made a mistake. That's frustrating, unfortunate, and inconvenient, but it's not a catastrophe! I don't like making mistakes, but I can take it. I really would like things to go perfectly, but that's impossible. A mistake does not make me a bad parent. I'm still a worthy person. I can work to avoid yelling in the future. If I slip, I'm still okay."

You may still feel annoyed and disappointed after telling yourself these things. But you won't feel angry, discouraged, and stressed. You will have changed your feelings and emotions by changing your beliefs. Furthermore, you are more likely to decide to change your behavior. By choosing a belief that leads to a more constructive way of dealing with the situation, you have reminded yourself that you are in charge.

Most activating events are not catastrophes. It's more helpful to think of them as simply unfortunate and inconvenient. Believe you can meet the challenges of life. Make the assumption that you are worthwhile even when your behavior leaves something to be desired.

The skills for building self-esteem can help you replace irrational beliefs with rational ones. A sense of humor and a willingness to accept yourself as you are can help you resist the tendency to give yourself commands. Humor and self-acceptance can also help you keep your perspective and avoid catastrophizing. Instead of stopping yourself with "can't-stand-it-itis," use self-affirmation to remind yourself that you can handle life's challenges. Instead of condemning yourself, make a habit of self-appreciation and self-encouragement.

Don't expect to master these skills overnight. That would be an irrational expectation! But with practice you can learn to catch yourself thinking irrationally and to choose less stressful beliefs.

Helping Your Children Deal with Stress

Children express tension in a variety of ways. Dr. Ronald R. Rubenzer lists the following as warning signs of excessive stress in children:

1. Sudden, dramatic increase or decrease in effort in school

2. Major change in attitude/temperament (irritability, lack of enthusiasm, carelessness)

3. Withdrawal or outbursts

4. Hyperactive behavior (fidgeting, nervous tics, jumping from task to task, difficulty concentrating)

5. Complaints of fatigue and vague illnesses

6. Difficulty sleeping

7. Stomachaches/headaches

8. Drug use/abuse

9. Increase in allergic/asthmatic attacks

10. Avoidance of school or testing situations by direct refusal or convenient illnesses[4]

Other common symptoms of stress include loss of appetite or excessive eating, nail biting, stuttering, not doing chores.

If you observe any of these stress symptoms in your children, you can help. Ask if anything is bothering them. Use reflective listening skills.* Be understanding—try to imagine what life is like for them.

---

*These are reviewed in the appendix and discussed in Chapter 5.

Remember, the same things that discourage children contribute to stress and tension:

- unreasonable demands
- unrealistic expectations
- overconcern with achievement

The same kind of encouragement that builds children's self-esteem will help them cope with stress.

Our children will never live in a stress-free environment. However, with our guidance, they can learn to regulate stress. We can

- help children establish realistic goals
- encourage any effort, attempt, or sign of progress
- create an atmosphere of belonging and acceptance
- help children become contributing members of the family
- help children develop relaxation skills
- listen for feelings and give feedback

Helping Children Cope with Major Changes

Today's children encounter potentially stressful circumstances with increasing frequency. It's important to be aware of the effect common family stresses can have on your children and to learn what you can do to help.

New baby in the family. Even happy events can be experienced as stressful. The birth or adoption of a child brings many changes to the family, and wherever there is change, there is potential for stress. Siblings may eagerly anticipate the birth of a new baby, but the event itself can bring feelings of jealousy and insecurity.

Make time for the children. Encourage their participation in caring for the new baby. Use listening skills, giving each

The birth of a new baby can bring feelings of jealousy and insecurity.

child your undivided attention at some point during the day. If children can express their feelings and maintain a sense of belonging, they will adjust more quickly.

Moving to a new community. Because moving calls for many adjustments, it can be stressful for families. Parents need to remember that leaving friends, school, and familiar surroundings can be hard on children. Children are flexible, but they do experience loss and may feel a lack of control over their lives. They may need help understanding and accepting these feelings. Sharing your own feelings may encourage them to do the same.

Another way to help children make the transition is by asking them to help you learn about the new community. This encourages their support and involvement.

Job loss. Children tend to assume the adult world never changes. When a parent loses a job, that illusion is shattered. Children may experience anxiety and insecurity. They are likely to pick up on their parents' fears. If the unemployed parent loses self-esteem or becomes depressed, this will add to the children's anxiety.

Children often ask, "What's going to happen?" Be open with them. Let them know there may be some temporary changes requiring their cooperation, but reassure them that the situation is not likely to be permanent. Discuss family finances with them so they will know how the change in income will affect them. The family meeting provides a good forum for such a discussion. You may want to explore alternatives for coping with the change in income.

Serious illness of a family member. Children are often confused and anxious when a parent or other close family member is ill. Withholding facts from them may increase their anxiety. Sensing your worry, they may magnify the seriousness of the illness. Consider allowing them to sit in on a conference with the doctor. Help them understand how the illness affects what the family member is currently able to do.

Talk to them honestly about the nature of the illness and ask for their cooperation. If it is a long-term or chronic illness, the children need to know how the household routine will be affected. Let them know if they will be expected to carry increased responsibilities or if there will be any changes in the family budget. The family meeting is a good place to discuss these matters.

Death of a family member. Adults and children alike find the loss of a family member difficult to accept. Parents who try to shield their children are only compounding the difficulty. Children need to learn to understand the transition from life to death. Allow them to participate in the ritual of the funeral and in the grieving.

It may be difficult for grieving adults to discuss the death with children. But sharing feelings can bring the family closer together and accelerate healing for everyone.

Children who lose a parent through death may become fearful about the future. In attempting to deal with their feelings, they may exhibit behavior changes. For example, the normally cheerful child may become withdrawn and refuse to interact with friends. The good student may refuse to study and begin acting out in class. Behavior changes are a normal response to loss and will fade as the child works through the grieving process.

Knowing the five stages of the grieving process—denial, anger, bargaining, depression, and acceptance—will help you understand temporary behavior changes in your children. For a detailed discussion of these five stages, see Elisabeth Kübler-Ross's *On Death and Dying.*[5]

Resist the temptation to urge your children to put the death behind them and get on with their lives before they have had a chance to complete their grieving. Each family member will move through the grieving process at his or her own speed. Reassure children that it is all right to feel the way they do. Otherwise, they may feel they have to pretend to accept the death before they're ready.

Divorce. During separation and divorce, the amount of stress children experience depends to a large degree on

- how parents communicate with them about the divorce

- how parents deal with each other, friends, and the extended family in the children's presence

- the amount of immediate change

Children's stress is reduced when the divorcing partners deal with their problems and disagreements privately. Also, parents need to agree not to encourage the children to take sides. It can be stressful for a child to believe that the only way to retain the love of one parent is to give up loyalty to the other.

If a divorce results in children no longer seeing one parent, there may be feelings of abandonment. The children may not understand the reasons why the parent left and may feel responsible. They may misinterpret the custodial parent's anger and think it is being directed toward them.

Children who continue to have contact with both parents will also experience stress. They sometimes must move back and forth between two homes where there are different patterns, rules, and expectations.

Whether they continue to have contact with both parents or not, children who have been through a divorce will experience grief. They can be expected to go through the five stages of the grieving process in much the same way as the child who has lost a parent through death.

Financial situations often get worse for the custodial parent. A mother who previously did not work outside the home, for example, may immediately need to seek employment or return to school for career training. These changes may put additional stress on the children.

Often one or both parents remarry, sometimes before the children have fully adjusted to their parents' divorce. Children may become jealous or feel insecure when this happens, or even when a parent brings a dating partner into the home. They may fear that your love for this new person will replace your love for them. You can reassure children by explaining that the love between a man and a woman is different from the love between parent and child. The two kinds of love need not compete with each other. Listen for feelings and encourage the children to talk with you about these two kinds of love. Through open discussion jealousy, guilt, and resentment can be reduced and trust increased. Also, spend some time alone with your children so they won't feel left out.

Good Communication is the Key

Children need to be kept informed about what's going on when major family changes are in progress. It is better for them to know the worst than to have to imagine the worst. They have a right to know about changes that affect them.

But don't burden them unnecessarily by trying to use them as counselors. Acknowledge your own painful feelings and give them the chance to acknowledge theirs. Encourage them to talk freely with you about things that trouble them.

The Importance of Relaxation

Parents and children alike can benefit from learning to relax. Tension, anxiety, and fear diminish when you relax. You feel a sense of peace and well-being. Because relaxation helps overcome the negative effects of stress, it helps your body fight disease. In a state of relaxation, the heart rate becomes slower and more regular, breathing becomes deeper and more even, and muscles loosen and relax.

It takes time and practice to create a state of relaxation. But through simple exercises you can learn to relax any time, any place. You can also share these exercises with your children.

You can learn to relax any time, any place.

Deep Breathing

Deep breathing is the simplest relaxation technique to learn and to practice. When you experience stress, your breathing often becomes shallow and rapid. When you are relaxed, your breathing is deeper and slower. By taking just twenty seconds to practice deep breathing you can help reduce the effects of the stress you are experiencing.

Find a quiet place where you will not be disturbed. Sit in a comfortable chair, preferably one with a straight back. Take off your shoes. Sit back in the chair. Breathe in and out, slowly and deeply, but naturally. Breathe deeply into your abdomen, so that your stomach swells each time you inhale. Say the word relax *each time you breathe out. As you breathe in and out, slowly, deeply, and naturally, you will begin to feel tension drain from your body.*

When you learn what it feels like to be deeply relaxed, you will be able to recreate this state any time you choose. Then when you find yourself in a tense situation, you can use deep breathing to reduce stress. But don't restrict your practice of deep breathing to stressful times. Schedule some time each day to experience this form of relaxation.

Muscle Relaxation

Relaxation can also be achieved by tensing and then relaxing the muscle groups of the body. When you purposely tense muscles, you raise the muscle tension to above-normal levels. When you quickly release the tension, the muscles relax.

Begin by making a tight fist. You should feel tension in your hand, over your knuckles, and in your lower arm. Hold the level of tension for five to seven seconds, counting to yourself. Then quickly release the tension. Be sure to release it abruptly, not gradually. Pay close attention to the physical sensations associated with tensing and then relaxing a muscle group, so that you will know what deep relaxation feels like.

Next, tense and then relax your other hand and forearm. One by one, tense and then relax the other major muscle groups in the body: biceps (front muscle, upper arm), triceps (back muscle, upper arm), head area (eyes, face, throat), shoulder muscles, upper back muscles, lower back muscles, chest muscles, stomach muscles, pelvic muscles, buttocks, upper leg muscles, calf and shin muscles, feet and toes.

With each set of muscles, hold the tension five to seven seconds, notice how the tension feels, and then quickly release it. Feel the muscle deeply relax. After tensing and releasing a muscle group, leave it as relaxed and still as possible.

This simple, effective relaxation procedure can help you become aware of muscle tension that signals stress. Relaxing tense muscles can also reduce anxiety.[6]

You can share relaxation exercises
with your family.

"The Relaxation Response"

Another form of relaxation, developed by Herbert Benson, focuses on repeating a word or phrase that has soothing qualities for you. Mentally repeating the word or phrase in a slow, rhythmic way helps you focus your mind whenever distracting thoughts occur. Positive associations and feelings about the word or phrase take the place of tension-producing thoughts and concerns.

Benson calls this "the relaxation response." His instructions for practicing it are presented below. It is easiest to do this exercise in a quiet, calm environment with few distractions.

1. Sit quietly in a comfortable position.

2. Close your eyes.

3. Deeply relax all your muscles, beginning at your feet and progressing up to your face. Keep them relaxed.

4. Breathe through your nose. Become aware of your breathing. As you breathe out, say the word "ONE" silently to yourself. . . . Breathe easily and naturally.

5. Continue for 10-20 minutes. You may open your eyes to check the time, but do not use an alarm. When you finish, sit quietly for several minutes, at first with your eyes closed and later with your eyes opened. Do not stand up for a few minutes.

6. Do not worry about whether you are successful in achieving a deep level of relaxation. Maintain a passive attitude and permit relaxation to occur at its own pace. When distracting thoughts occur, try to ignore them by not dwelling upon them and return to repeating "ONE.". . . Practice the technique once or twice daily, but not within two hours after eating, since the digestive processes seem to interfere with the elicitation of the Relaxation Response.[7]

Visual Imagery

Another form of relaxation involves using a single visual image. Choose an image that is meaningful to you, one that suggests peace, strength, or a calm, quiet happiness. A mountain, a pool of water, or the ocean are images some people associate with serenity and peace.

First, relax by concentrating on your breathing. Deeply inhale and exhale. Visualize the strengthening energies of life traveling into your body and filling your lungs as you inhale. Then envision undesirable emotions and difficulties leaving your body as you exhale.

Now visualize the image of your choice "in your mind's eye" with as much detail as possible. Begin to feel the qualities you associate with the image. Hold onto these feelings for as long as you can before emerging from your state of relaxation.

The Quieting Response

Emergencies evoke a typical response in the human body: release of adrenalin, tense muscles, faster breathing, and a quicker heart rate. Sometimes referred to as the fight-or-flight reaction, these physiological changes give us the strength we would need to fight or to run to safety if, say, we were to encounter a tiger in the wild.

The body also has a normal quieting response. But under the potentially stressful conditions of modern life, the "emergency response" is sometimes activated so often that our bodies start to ignore this natural quieting response. Excessive, prolonged tension begins to seem normal.

Quieting Response (QR) training helps you to regain the capacity you once had to recover quickly from excessive stress. (Even children can lose this capacity.) The quieting response becomes an automatic part of your body's response mechanism, freeing you from the pattern of repeated emergency responses which may have been keeping you tense.

Excessive tension
can begin to seem normal.

Here's a simplified version of QR you or your children can use when you experience tension, annoyance, or anxiety, or notice any acceleration of your breathing:

1. Smile inwardly and give yourself the suggestion, "alert mind—calm body."

2. Inhale easily, taking a deep breath.

3. While exhaling, let jaw, tongue, and shoulders go limp, feeling a wave of heaviness and warmth flow to the toes.

4. Resume normal activity.[8]

Making Relaxation a Priority

You may find it difficult to schedule time for relaxation exercises. But once you experience their benefits, you will want to make relaxation a priority. When you are relaxed, you sleep better and have more energy. Relaxation refreshes you. It leaves you ready to get on with your work and other interests, better able to find new ways to interpret situations that in the past have been stress-producing. Taking time for yourself should include taking time to relax.

Conclusion

Dealing effectively with stress is a matter of learning the skills and attitudes that will help you cope with changes and challenges. Just taking the attitude that you *can* cope is one of the most useful things you can do. That should be easier now that you know you're not at the mercy of your strong upset feelings. Being realistic is also important—it isn't effective to try to command reality to be a certain way. And you can't cope with change effectively by denying that it has happened. Accept reality as it is and recognize that you don't have to get upset about it. Accept yourself, keep your sense of humor, and let go of tension.

Being realistic and accepting is also the best way to help your children cope with potentially stressful situations. If difficult or painful changes are taking place in the family, it's best not to deny or cover up the reality of what's going on—give your children the information they need and accept the reality of their feelings. Knowing that you love and accept them and having the opportunity to express their griefs and anxieties will give them the confidence they need to face the challenges life brings.

Notes

1. Albert Ellis and Robert A. Harper, *A New Guide to Rational Living* (Englewood Cliffs, N.J.: Prentice Hall, 1975), 36.

2. This term was coined by Albert Ellis in *How to Live With and Without Anger* (New York: Readers' Digest Press, 1977),78.

3. Ellis and Harper, 41.

4. Ronald R. Rubenzer, "Stress: Causes and Cures in Gifted Kids," *Gifted Children Monthly* 7 (March 1986): 2. Used by permission of *Gifted Children Monthly*.

5. Elisabeth Kübler-Ross, *On Death and Dying* (New York: Macmillan, 1969), 38-137.

6. Edmund Jacobson, *You Must Relax* (New York: McGraw Hill, 1962).

7. Herbert Benson, *The Relaxation Response* (New York: William Morrow, 1975).

8. For those who desire to become proficient at the Quieting Response, we recommend that you obtain Charles F. Stroebel's *Quieting Reflex Training for Adults,* available from BMA Audiocassette Publications, 200 Park Ave. S., New York, NY 10003. A program for children is also available on audiocassette: Elizabeth Stroebel's *Kiddie QR: A Choice for Children,* which can be ordered from the QR Institute, 119 Forest Drive, Wethersfield, CT 06109.

Activity for the Week

Practice at least one relaxation exercise every day this week.

Family Enrichment Activity

Part 1. The Stresses in Your Life

1. List the stresses in your life, from the most to the least stressful.

2. Think of a plan for reducing each stress.

Stress: _____

Plan: _____

_____

_____

Stress: _____

Plan: _____

_____

_____

Stress: _____

Plan: _____

_____

_____

Stress: _____

Plan: _____

_____

_____

Stress: _____

Plan: _____

_____

_____

3. In a week, check your progress.

Family Enrichment Activity

Part 2. The Stresses on Your Children

1. List your children from the oldest to the youngest.

2. List the stresses on each child.

3. Think about the ways you may have contributed to the stress. Then list one thing you can do to reduce the stress or to help the child cope with it.

Child's name: _____

Stress 1: _____

Plan for helping: _____

_____

_____

Stress 2: _____

Plan for helping: _____

_____

_____

Child's name: _____

Stress 1: _____

Plan for helping: _____

_____

_____

Stress 2: _____

Plan for helping: _____

_____

_____

(continued)

Family Enrichment Activity

Child's name: _____

Stress 1: _____

Plan for helping: _____

_____

_____

Stress 2: _____

Plan for helping: _____

_____

_____

4. In a week, check your progress.

Points to Remember

1. Stress is the physical and emotional response we experience when we view an event as upsetting.

2. Our beliefs determine whether we feel an event is upsetting.

3. We can choose to see upsetting events that are beyond our control as minor irritations and release them from our attention.

4. Beliefs that involve commanding ourselves or reality to be a certain way are irrational.

5. We can lead more satisfying lives with less stress when we have realistic beliefs about life.

6. We can help children learn to regulate stress by
   - helping them set realistic goals
   - encouraging any effort, attempt, or sign of progress
   - creating an atmosphere of belonging and acceptance
   - helping them become contributing members of the family
   - helping them develop relaxation skills
   - listening for feelings and giving feedback

7. Children need information and a chance to talk about their feelings during times of change.

8. Relaxation helps us overcome the negative effects of stress by slowing the heart rate, deepening breathing, and loosening muscles.

9. Some of the ways we can create a state of relaxation include deep breathing, muscle relaxation, "the relaxation response," visual imagery, and the Quieting Response.

CHAPTER FIVE

Making
Decisions
as a Family

Finding Time to Talk

Many families today seldom sit down together, even for a meal. And in some families, when everyone does get together, the T.V. set is often the focus of attention. Opportunities to talk things over as a family may be rare.

But discussing family plans and concerns as a group offers many potential benefits. Getting together regularly helps create a feeling of unity. Taking time to listen to one another communicates that everyone is important. When family members know that their views count, they have a greater feeling of belonging. And meeting regularly provides an opportunity to make plans and decisions as a family.

Taking a Democratic Approach

In some families, the parents make all the decisions in isolation. But effective parents involve their children. They take a democratic approach and give children a say in decisions that affect them. This communicates respect and gives the children valuable practice in making decisions. Using the democratic process in family meetings helps children learn to make responsible choices.

Family meetings offer parents an excellent opportunity to model good communication and problem-solving skills for their children. When children learn to listen to all sides of an issue, they realize that blaming other people doesn't resolve a conflict. Through group brainstorming, they discover that there are many possible solutions to a problem.

One of the chief benefits of family democracy is that children become more responsible about carrying out agreements. They also complain less about how things are being done, since the decisions reached are at least partly theirs. They know their views have been heard. Their attitude is more likely to be cooperative and respectful.

Setting Up Family Meetings

For those who have never held family meetings, here are some brief guidelines for setting them up:

You'll want to choose a time for your meeting when everyone can come and a place that's free of distractions. Post this information in an obvious place—on the refrigerator or a bulletin board, for example. You may also want to post a sheet of paper for family members to list items they'd like to talk about. Parents or older siblings can write down items suggested by younger children. This list then becomes your agenda.

Many families prefer a formal approach and find that the following format works well:

1. Read and discuss the minutes of the previous meeting.

2. Discuss any issues left unresolved last time.

3. Consider each new item on the agenda.

4. After discussing as many agenda items as time allows, summarize the meeting by reviewing decisions, agreements, and commitments. Then evaluate the meeting by asking members how they feel about the decisions reached.

5. Agree on a time for the next meeting.

Feeling Reluctant

The idea of operating a family democratically strikes some parents as radical. The autocratic approach to parenting, in which a parent's word is law, has been deeply ingrained in our culture. Parents who have control as a priority may feel threatened at the prospect of sharing decision making with the rest of the family.

Furthermore, it takes time and energy to hold meetings and listen to your children's ideas. It seems easier and faster just to make the decisions alone. Meeting formally to discuss family concerns can seem stiff, awkward, unnatural. It's no wonder the suggestion to hold regular family meetings often meets with resistance!

It takes time to develop new patterns of communication within a family and to acquire the leadership skills that make meetings go smoothly. Many parents hold a few family meetings while they are taking a *STEP* or *STEP/Teen* course. But then, before they've had time to get comfortable with the process or develop the skills to make meetings a success, they run up against difficulties, get discouraged, and quit.

Following are suggestions for addressing challenges parents commonly encounter during family meetings.

Troubleshooting Guide

Challenge 1: Your spouse or one or more of your children resists the idea of holding family meetings.

What You Can Do:
Emphasize the positive. If, in the past, your family has had meetings chiefly in response to crises or discipline situations, children may think a meeting means lecture time! It may take time for family members to learn that calling a family meeting doesn't mean someone has done something

Your spouse may resist the idea
of holding family meetings.

wrong. Let them know that, from now on, meetings will be a time for the family to share, cooperate, make plans, and decide things.

Make participation voluntary. Begin meeting with those members who are willing to attend. By letting individuals know it is their choice whether or not to attend, you communicate respect. The message that "This is an opportunity to be involved in making family plans, expressing concerns, and solving problems" will eventually get across to those who stay away. Make a special effort at another time to reassure those who don't attend family meetings that they are valued.

Challenge 2: The family has difficulty finding a good time to meet.

What You Can Do:

Finding a good meeting time may not be easy. Some families say, "You don't know how busy we all are—no one is ever home!" This common complaint is sometimes an excuse, just another way of saying, "We choose not to make the effort." It should be possible to find a time when everyone can come. (This is important, even though attendance is voluntary. Everyone has a contribution to make and everyone's presence is valuable.) Consider meeting on a weekend morning if you can't find a specific weekday night that works for your family. If mealtime is the only time available, have your meal first, clear the table, and then begin the meeting. That way, the meal itself won't distract people from the business at hand.

Challenge 3: Family members get frustrated because the meetings don't start on time or seem to drag on and on.

What You Can Do:

Starting and ending the meeting on time is a way of showing mutual respect. If meetings repeatedly begin later than scheduled, members tend to arrive later and later. This can be frustrating for members who are on time. To avoid this problem, agree the meeting will begin on time whether or not all members—including parents—are present, and stick to that.

Establish a time limit when you begin the meeting. A family meeting with younger children may last only ten minutes. An upper limit for families with older children might be forty-five minutes to an hour. At the end of the scheduled time, if there are issues that haven't yet been discussed, members can decide whether to table those issues until the next meeting.

Challenge 4: The meetings have a negative tone.

What You Can Do:

Get off to a good start. You will want to have a positive focus for all your family meetings, but particularly for the first ones. Regardless of the backlog of issues to be resolved, it's a good idea to limit the agenda for the first few

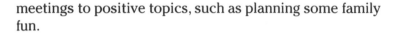

meetings to positive topics, such as planning some family fun.

Many families begin every meeting by having each person share something new and good in his or her life. This kind of sharing lifts people's spirits and sets an excellent tone for the rest of the meeting. What's new and good doesn't have to be something big—any recent event you felt good about will do.

Here is a communication exercise that uses the "new and good" approach:

Ask the first person to share something new and good. Ask the next person, before sharing, to summarize what the first person said. Then have the first person indicate whether she or he was heard accurately. Next, the second person takes a turn sharing. Continue the process until each person has had a turn.

Avoid a negative tone
in your family meetings.

Use encouragement. Lay the framework for mutual respect and cooperation by using encouragement. It has a powerful effect on the tone of meetings. Remind the group that you appreciate them. Ask members to say what they like about each other. Remember to focus on efforts and contributions, no matter how small.

Focus on goals and solutions. Perhaps the most widespread faulty belief about family meetings is, "We've got some problems and the family meeting will solve them." Family meetings can solve problems, but they won't work if they are undertaken in anger or as the only effort to solve major challenges.

Meetings are most effective when they focus on what can be done, rather than on why things aren't working. In general, it's best to focus meetings on things a family needs to decide, not on an individual's behavior. Family meetings are not meant to serve as a forum for parents to preach, scold, or impose rules. Nagging, criticizing, threatening, and lecturing are also out of place. An effective chairperson won't allow anyone to call names, complain about things that are over and done with, interrupt, or make assumptions about how another person is feeling.

Discourage griping. If a meeting seems to be turning into a gripe session, refocus it. Turn to a discussion of what is good about the family or about the ideas that have been presented. Then ask members to brainstorm ideas for improving the immediate situation.

Don't dwell on the past. Dwelling on the past can have a negative effect on the tone of a meeting. We can't affect the past, only the present. What is happening now is the appropriate subject for discussion. The leader can help group members focus on the present and the future:

Francesca: I never get what I want! You all decide things, and I have no say.

Leader: You're angry because you feel you've been treated unfairly in the past. How can we include you more?

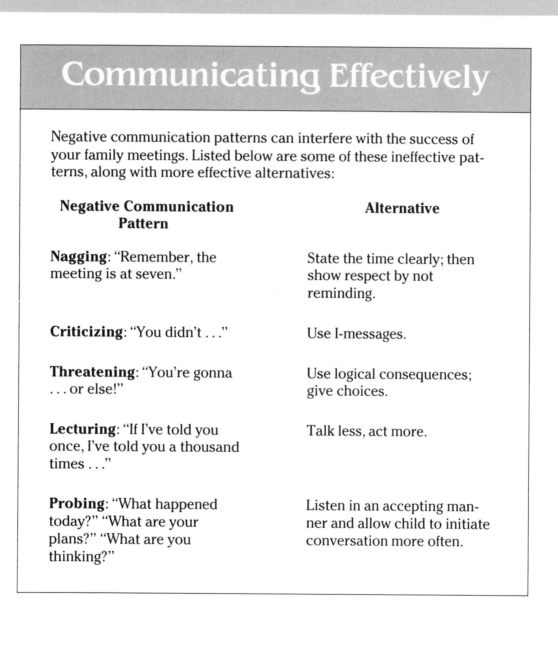

Communicating Effectively

Negative communication patterns can interfere with the success of your family meetings. Listed below are some of these ineffective patterns, along with more effective alternatives:

Negative Communication Pattern	Alternative
Nagging: "Remember, the meeting is at seven."	State the time clearly; then show respect by not reminding.
Criticizing: "You didn't . . ."	Use I-messages.
Threatening: "You're gonna . . . or else!"	Use logical consequences; give choices.
Lecturing: "If I've told you once, I've told you a thousand times . . ."	Talk less, act more.
Probing: "What happened today?" "What are your plans?" "What are you thinking?"	Listen in an accepting manner and allow child to initiate conversation more often.

Challenge 5: The discussion wanders off the topic or gets sidetracked, time runs out, and everyone ends up feeling that nothing is being accomplished.

What You Can Do:

Structure your meetings. To be effective, a family meeting needs structure. If you're attempting to solve a problem at the meeting, the following approach can provide that structure. It involves *exploring alternatives* by going through these steps:

1. *Understand and clarify the problem.*

In this step, I-messages, reflective listening, and open-ended questions help each person understand what the others feel and think.

2. *Explore alternatives through brainstorming.*

When a family brainstorms, all ideas are considered, no matter how ridiculous some may seem at first. If an idea is rejected immediately, creativity is stifled. During brainstorming, just list the ideas as they're suggested.

3. *Evaluate proposed alternatives.*

Discuss all the ideas suggested. Ask the children to give their opinions of an idea. Then give yours. Use sentences such as

> "I like this idea because . . ."

> "I'm uncomfortable with this idea because . . ."

4. *Choose a solution.*

Decide together which idea or ideas to use. Some ideas may be modified or combined.

5. *Make a commitment and set a time to evaluate.*

Summarize what you've agreed on. Say that you're willing to keep the agreement, and ask if everyone else is too. If anyone says, "I'll try," say, "When I hear people say 'I'll try,' I'm not convinced they want to keep the agreement. Are you willing to keep the agreement or shall we talk some more?"

Discourage use of the word "try"
in commitment statements.

You may need to build a consequence into the agreement. "We all forget sometimes. What would be a fair consequence if you forget to keep the agreement, and what would be a fair consequence if I forget?"

Propose the agreement as an experiment you will do for a certain length of time—usually until the next meeting. With younger children, you may want to talk about how it's going within a couple of days. Remember, it's unrealistic to assume that agreements will always be kept.

Agreements can be written down and signed so everyone knows what is expected. Then the agreement can be posted in a place where everyone can see it. You may want to have a secretary who keeps a record of family decisions and posts agreements.

Stay on task. Family meetings run more smoothly when someone acts as chairperson and takes responsibility for structuring the discussion. The chairperson needs to keep the family on task by making sure they stick to the agenda topics and stay within time limits. For example, the leader can say, "Let's spend five minutes talking about this. Who'd like to start?" If the discussion wanders from the topic, the leader can say, "We seem to be getting off the topic. Let's get back to our discussion of bedtimes."

Avoid sidetracking. Sometimes someone will try to side-track a discussion, perhaps because that person doesn't want to deal with a particular problem. Sidetracking may involve making excuses or accusing. The leader's job is to see to it that everyone sticks to the point.

Avoid sidetracking.

Challenge 6: A child feels the parents are "ganging up" on him or her at the meeting.

What You Can Do:

If you have a problem that involves only one child, you may wish to discuss the problem in private, with only one parent present, rather than put it on the agenda for a family meeting. If you do decide to discuss it at a family meeting, don't begin looking for solutions right away. First, ask the child to talk about how she or he feels about the issue, and use reflective listening.

Challenge 7: Family members can't agree on what to do about a problem.

What You Can Do:

Family members won't always be able to reach an agreement right away. Sometimes negotiations break down—no matter what others do or say, someone is unwilling to cooperate. On a hot topic, emotions may be running too high. Or the group may just get bogged down. If the problem is minor, it can be tabled. Ask everyone to bring a solution to the next meeting. But if an issue has to be resolved right away, tell the children this and ask them if they want to agree temporarily to abide by majority rule—or, make a temporary decision yourself. You could say, "It seems we are not ready to agree on this, but something has to be done now. So I guess we will _____ (state the decision)." If anyone has come up with a better idea by the next meeting, he or she can suggest a new agreement at that time.

Challenge 8: Discussion time is monopolized by one or two people.

What You Can Do:

Family meetings become stale and unproductive when only one or two people express feelings, concerns, ideas, and solutions. Redirecting may be necessary to get others involved. You can encourage wider participation by asking, "What do the rest of you think about this?" By asking,

Watch that family meetings don't become dominated by one or two people.

"Does anyone else feel this way?" you can help family members become aware that their questions and concerns are shared by others. Members who are reluctant to speak up may need some individual encouragement. Ask, "What's your opinion, Carl?" or, "We haven't heard from you, Barbara—what do you think about this?"

Challenge 9: Children don't like to come because parents dominate the meetings.

What You Can Do:
Make sure children's issues get attention. If meetings deal largely with issues parents bring up, younger family members will lose interest. So when planning the agenda for a family meeting, ask everyone to suggest items for discussion. Children may not, at first, have pinpointed what

they want to talk about. Ask them if they have something they would like to bring up. If they don't, you may need to think of topics that will interest them. After a few meetings, they will start to have their own ideas and to place items on the agenda.

Give children responsibilities. A parent usually assumes the role of chairperson at first. However, it's important to give children the opportunity to lead as soon as possible. This says to them, "You are capable." Even a young child can chair a meeting or co-lead it with another person. Be careful not to judge the child's performance against that of a more experienced leader. You can get younger children involved in other ways as well—let them assist by handing out agendas, posting memos, or tape-recording the minutes.

Get children involved in coming up with solutions. When you explore alternatives through brainstorming, draw out your children. Ask them for their suggestions first. Add your ideas only if necessary—the more involved the children are in proposing solutions, the more likely they will be to carry them out.

You might explain brainstorming to a young child as follows: "Let's think of as many ideas as we can. I'll list them. Let's not talk about any of them until we're all through. Okay?"

If the children are slow to catch on, your ideas can serve as examples to stimulate their thinking. You may want to make a few extreme suggestions to help them see that any idea is acceptable, no matter how farfetched.

Let children know you hear them by using reflective listening. Children will lose interest in the meetings if they feel you aren't really listening to them. Two guidelines for effective listening bear repeating:

- Treat your child as you treat your best friend.

- Show mutual respect by accepting your child's feelings.

When people communicate, it's important to understand feelings as well as thoughts. Using the reflective listening skills taught in the earlier *STEP* programs, you can let your child know that you understand the feelings behind the words.

Suppose your child says angrily, "I don't like to visit Uncle Harry. He makes fun of me!" You might respond, "You feel angry because you think Uncle Harry treats you badly," reflecting in your own words both the feelings and the circumstances that led to them: the child was angry about being teased.

The format "You feel _____ because _____ " is very useful when you practice reflective listening. As you become more comfortable with this type of response, you can use other leads: "Seems like," "Sounds like," "I hear you saying," or whatever seems natural to you.

Keep your responses open, and be sure that your words are interchangeable with what the child has said. This communicates, "I understand." Lectures, reminders, reassurances, advice, and too many questions are "closed" responses— they turn off the child because they indicate you don't really hear the feelings.

The purpose of reflective listening is to let a person know she or he is being heard. Here is an example:

Parent: Let's talk about the chores. They're not getting done.

Child: I don't want to talk about chores. I had a lot of schoolwork this week.

Parent: You're feeling overloaded with schoolwork?

Child: Yes. My report was due and it took a lot of time.

The conversation hasn't yet dealt with chores. However, the parent has given an open response, making it more likely that the dialogue will proceed in a constructive way. The open response acknowledges the child's right to the feelings by demonstrating that the parent understands them.

After the child's concern about schoolwork is acknowledged, the conversation can return to the agenda item, with the focus on possible solutions:

Parent: I understand the report took a lot of time. How can the chores be a part of your schedule this week?

Reflective listening helps identify the issue. For the parent, the undone chores are the issue. But for the child, too much schoolwork is the issue. Reflective listening can help parents deal with the child's concern; it also increases the likelihood that the issue of chores will be resolved.

In contrast, here is a conversation in which the parent gives a closed response:

Parent: Let's talk about the chores. They're not getting done.

Child: I don't want to talk about chores. I had a lot of schoolwork this week.

Parent: I don't care if you did. The garbage has to be taken out. It's your job.

Child: One week I don't take out the garbage and you get bent out of shape!

In this conversation, the parent's closed response puts the child on the defensive and stifles communication. It doesn't get the garbage taken out, and it has a negative effect on the relationship.

A closed response says to the child, "I don't accept your right to feel the way you do." It communicates lack of understanding. How the child feels—not the fact that the garbage isn't being taken out—is the immediate concern. Unless the child's feelings are addressed, the chores issue can't be settled. In addition, closed communication says, "I don't care about your feelings or what you have to do in your life." Would you treat your best friend that way?

Challenge 10: Someone disrupts meetings repeatedly.

What You Can Do:

If someone is disrupting the meetings, use I-messages to give them feedback: "When you interrupt, I feel concerned because I can't pay attention to what the others are saying." If the disruptive behavior continues, as a logical consequence you could ask that person to leave the meeting and come back when he or she is ready to cooperate.

Conclusion

The immediate benefits of family meetings include improved communication, more effective ways to deal with conflict, and time to plan together. There are also long-term benefits. If you listen to your children in family meetings and let them know their opinions count, they will develop feelings of self-worth and confidence in their decision making. The skills they practice in the family meeting help prepare them to make decisions that affect their lives and the lives of others.

New patterns take time. The people in your family will not start to behave differently right away, simply because you have family meetings. You may find it takes several weeks to establish a familiar, effective pattern for your meetings. Be patient with your progress and concentrate on what is going well. Don't expect your meetings to be perfect. Be sure to offer encouragement and keep your expectations realistic. Patience and persistence will pay off!

Activity for the Week

Take up the issue of stress at a family meeting. Ask, "What are some of the major stresses in this family?" If the family has gone through any big changes recently, ask whether anyone has feelings about the changes they'd like to share. Find out whether others share those feelings and concerns.

After the major stresses have been determined, ask, "What can we do to reduce these stresses?" Explore alternatives.

Family Enrichment Activity

1. What has gone well in your family meetings in the past?_____

_____

_____

_____

_____

_____

2. What hasn't gone well? _____

_____

_____

_____

_____

_____

3. List three specific steps you can take to improve your family meetings. _____

_____

_____

_____

_____

Points to Remember

1. Effective parents give children a say in decisions that affect them.

2. Plan an agenda for your family meetings ahead of time, encouraging input from all family members.

3. Make participation in meetings voluntary.

4. Start and end meetings on time.

5. Approach problems that are brought up at meetings by exploring alternatives and making agreements.

6. Give your meetings a positive tone; focus on goals and solutions.

7. Put children's issues on the agenda, give them meeting responsibilities, and involve them in coming up with solutions.

8. To let family members know they have been heard, use reflective listening and keep your responses open.

9. At the end of a meeting, review the decisions, agreements, and commitments and ask members how they feel about the decisions reached.

10. Be patient with the family's progress—encouragement and realistic expectations are important.

CHAPTER SIX

Gentle Strength and Firm Love

Setting Limits

Like most parents, you probably have concerns about how to discipline your children effectively. If you've taken a *STEP* or *STEP/Teen* course, you've learned that an autocratic ("Do as I say because I say so") approach gives children too little freedom and not enough responsibility. On the other hand, permissiveness produces undisciplined children. So you're taking a democratic approach. You encourage your children to

- make decisions
- think for themselves
- be responsible
- care about and help other members of the family

But when things don't go well, it can be difficult to stick with the democratic approach. When your children get out of hand, autocratic methods can be appealing, particularly if you value control. You may begin to doubt yourself. "Am I being too soft or permissive?" you may wonder. "My friends seem to think I'm letting the kids walk all over me. How strict is strict enough?" The oft-heard advice to "show 'em who's boss" can be tempting. How can you respond?

The answer, of course, is that in a democratic family the parents are not "bosses." By treating your children as equals in human worth and dignity, you base your relationship with them on mutual respect.

Who's in charge, then? As the parent, you are. You guide your children and oversee their well-being. But your goal is to teach self-discipline, not to reward and punish your children in order to control them.

When your children get out of hand,
autocratic methods can be appealing.

Controlling the Situation, Not the Child

Many discipline approaches used in classrooms and homes attempt to control children. These approaches seem to work for a while, but they don't achieve lasting results. Most people—including children—don't like to be controlled.

Parents need to maintain control of the situation—not of the child. Controlling the situation means setting limits and giving choices within those limits. For example, when you're on the phone, you need quiet. If your children are noisy and it's inconvenient for you to go to another phone, give them a choice: quiet down or leave the room.

Attempts to control your child are likely to provoke rebellion. By providing guidelines and giving choices, you can instead enlist your child's cooperation and awaken a sense of responsibility.

Being Gentle, Yet Firm

You can help your children grow toward self-discipline by using gentle strength and firm love. Gentle strength means holding to the limits you set. Firm love involves expecting your children to respect those limits. Strength and firmness work best if they have a democratic foundation. This means giving your children choices within the limits you set. It also means treating children with respect.

Martin, age three, expects—and receives—whatever he requests for breakfast, no matter how many times he changes his mind while deciding. His parents sometimes throw out more than one bowl of cereal before Martin settles down to eat.

By permitting this behavior, Martin's parents teach him he can do whatever he chooses. To regain control of the situation, they can still give him choices, but within limits. For example, they may continue to let Martin choose his breakfast cereal—but with the understanding that once the milk is poured, the decision is final. If he chooses not to eat the cereal, it is removed from the table and Martin is told, in a firm but friendly tone, "I see you have decided not to eat breakfast. You'll be offered something else to eat at lunchtime."

Effective discipline requires you to be gentle and firm at the same time. Firmness is not to be confused with strictness. Strictness involves attempting to control children. Firmness means sticking to your own decisions.

Consider Carla. She tells her children, firmly but kindly, "I'll drive you to the movies if you're ready by 6:30. That will give me time to drop you off and get to my meeting." Again, her children have a choice: be ready to leave on time or miss the movie. (If her children are too young to be left home alone, she will need to have a sitter standing by.) Carla has made a decision and set limits. In order to show gentle strength, she needs to stick to her decision. If the children are late and she waits, she shows a lack of respect for herself. If she resorts to nagging, reminding, or threatening, she is showing disrespect for the children. She is being strict rather than firm.

To show children your love, remain firm on the limits you set. To give in or to fight is disrespectful.

Being Assertive

Using gentle strength and firm love sometimes requires you to be assertive. Being assertive means standing up for your own rights.

Being assertive is quite different from being aggressive. Aggressive parents are autocrats who make demands on children. Quite often they are angry. Assertive parents calmly but firmly state what they are and are not willing to do. Instead of making demands on the child, they assert their own rights.

Assertive parents calmly but firmly state
what they are and are not willing to do.

Parents' Rights

In their book *How to Deal with Your Acting-Up Teenager,*
Bayard and Bayard list the rights a parent typically wants:

The right to privacy.

*The right to my own relationships with my spouse
and friends.*

The right to be free of fear of violence.

The right to feel secure about my belongings.

The right to some time of my own.

The right to be treated with courtesy.

*The right to relationships that are two-way rather
than only one-way streets.*

The right to reasonable peace and quiet.

*The right to feel everyone is carrying his or her
weight and I am not supporting a freeloader.*

*The right to close up my house in the evening and
know that no one will come in after that.*[1]

All these rights are variations of the right to be treated with
respect.

Taking Time for Yourself

Often parents don't take time for themselves. But time for
yourself isn't just your right, it's a necessity. If you are married, you need not only time alone, but time with your
partner. If you are a single parent, you need time for yourself and your own social life.

It takes planning to arrange uninterrupted time for yourself,
particularly if your children are used to having you at their
beck and call. If your children are old enough to be left unat-
tended for a time, you might tell them, "I've decided that
every day at this time, I want to be by myself. I'll be going to
my bedroom for my quiet time. I would appreciate it if you
would respect my need for quiet. Then I'll come out to be

with you." If the children try to interrupt your private time, lock your door and don't come out! (Except in emergencies, of course, or to ensure the safety of young children. But remember, emergencies seldom occur.) If the children continue their attempt to interrupt, don't scold them or mention their lack of respect. Just ignore their behavior. If you're firm in your decision, they'll find out that interrupting you doesn't work, and they'll stop.

Some of us were raised with the belief that if parents—particularly mothers—take time for themselves, they are cheating their children. But that's an irrational belief. It is unrealistic for anyone to be on call twenty-four hours a day. Taking time for yourself is a positive way to care for yourself. Your family will benefit too—you will have more energy for them if you take some time off.

Lee Schnebly, in her self-help book *Out of Apples,* compares people's resources to apples in a barrel. If parents constantly attend to their children and ignore themselves, they

It takes planning to arrange uninterrupted time for yourself, particularly if your children are used to having you at their beck and call.

are soon "out of apples." Parents need to keep some "apples" for their own "nourishment." When you "monitor your supply of apples" by taking care of yourself, you model self-respect for your children and help them develop respect for you.[2]

The Skills of Assertive Parenting

Asserting your rights as a parent in a respectful way takes practice. Several important skills are described below, some of which may be familiar to you from *STEP* or *STEP/Teen.* Experiment to see what works best for you.

Communicating Expectations and Making Agreements

Parents sometimes set children up for misbehavior by failing to make clear what they expect. When your child does something unacceptable—comes home late for dinner, for example—you may interpret this as misbehavior. But if you've never discussed what your child is to do when an activity runs overtime, you may unknowingly have set the child up for misbehavior. Agreements made in advance, perhaps at a family meeting, help children live up to your expectations.

If an agreement has been reached and your child doesn't honor it, then the next time the child wants to do the same activity, you can say, "I'm sorry, but you didn't keep our agreement last time, so you can't do that today. You can try again tomorrow."

I-messages

I-messages clearly and firmly express how you feel about your child's behavior. They don't blame or criticize; they simply state how the behavior affects you.[3] I-messages are particularly effective when you own the problem.

An I-message generally has three parts:

1. Describe the behavior. "WHEN the tools are used and not returned to the toolbox, . . ."

2. State how you feel about the *consequences* the behavior produces for you. ". . . , I FEEL discouraged, . . ."

3. State the consequence of the behavior for you. " . . . BECAUSE I can't find them when I need them."

Using I-messages with logical consequences. When I-messages fail to produce results, you can follow up with a logical consequence. For example, you could refuse to allow the child who does not put the tools away to use them the next time she wants to. If this is ineffective, you could put a lock on the toolbox to protect your rights. But first you may want to see if other ways of gaining cooperation will work. For example, you could use one of the following approaches.

Using I-messages with "I'd appreciate" statements. Usually we suggest you not offer solutions in your I-messages. But if your child seems to need help figuring out a respectful solution, you may want to add an "I'd appreciate" statement. The I-message then has four parts:

1. When . . .

2. I feel . . .

3. because . . .

4. I'd appreciate it if . . .

Here are examples:

"WHEN the tools are used and not returned, I FEEL discouraged, BECAUSE I can't find them when I need them. I'D APPRECIATE it if, in the future, you would put them back in the toolbox."

"WHEN you're late, I FEEL worried BECAUSE something may have happened to you. I'D APPRECIATE it if, in the future, you would be home on time or call."

The "I'd appreciate" statement needs to be said in a firm but respectful way. Be prepared to use your reflective listening skills if the child fires an I-message back to you. In some cases you'll need to look for a mutually agreeable solution through negotiation.

Willingness and intention statements. These can be used to communicate expectations and consequences. They state what you are or are not willing to do, or what you intend or do not intend to do. Then it's up to your children to choose how to respond.

Here are examples:

"I'M WILLING to let you use the tools if you're willing to put them away in the toolbox afterwards."

"I'M WILLING to help you with your homework after you've given it your full effort."

"I'M NOT WILLING to make out the grocery list by myself."

"I'M NOT WILLING to permit the use of alcohol in our home."

"I INTEND to call the police if you sneak out at night because I care about you and I'm legally responsible for you."

"I INTEND to take some time for myself so I can rest up and spend some good time with you."

Whenever possible, change "I'm not willing" to "I'm willing." Positive statements are more likely to be received positively. Instead of saying, "I'm not willing to have your friends in the house because they don't follow the rules," say, with a positive tone, "I'm willing to allow your friends to visit if you're willing to see that they follow our house rules."

Brief Confrontations

Sometimes you need to be firmer than the typical I-message allows. A brief, firm confrontation may be necessary.

Avoid confrontation at the time of the misbehavior, particularly if you're angry. Anger will only increase conflict. It's usually more effective to confront your child when you are calm and have had a chance to plan what you will say. Talk to the child in private. First, indicate that you have something to say and that when you're through, she or he may respond. Make eye contact. State your feelings clearly. Make it clear you're upset about the behavior, not about your child as a person.

Suppose your daughter continually leaves the bathroom in a mess. You say, "Linda, I want to talk to you. I'm upset about something and I want you to hear how I feel. When I'm finished, you can talk if you want to. But I want to be heard first. When I find the bathroom in a mess, I feel disgusted. The sink is full of hair and wet towels are all over

It's usually more effective
to confront your child when you are calm.

the floor. The tub is dirty, and I don't care to take a bath in a dirty tub. I want the bathroom cleaned up when you're through. I'm upset about this behavior, but I still love you."

A brief confrontation can lead to exploring alternatives. Even though you're not angry, your child may be. Be prepared to use reflective listening skills and be willing to negotiate.

Negotiation through Exploring Alternatives

When you have a problem with a child and no siblings are involved, you may want to negotiate privately with that child, one on one. (If both parents are present, the child may feel ganged up on.) You can go through the same steps used for exploring alternatives during a family meeting: understand and clarify the problem, brainstorm alternatives and evaluate them, choose a solution, make a commitment to it, and set a time to evaluate.

Exploring alternatives is an effective skill to use when negotiating to resolve conflicts. Choose a relaxed time. If tempers are flaring, nothing will be accomplished.

Sometimes, no matter what you do, the child is unwilling to cooperate, and negotiations break down. If possible, postpone further discussion until the child is in a more cooperative mood. If the problem has to be resolved right away, say so and make a temporary decision, to be reviewed after a certain period of time. In the meantime, invite the child to come up with a solution you both can live with. Then a new agreement can be made.

Task Trading

Task trading can be effective when a child does not follow through on agreements to do chores. It works like this:

- First, make a list of all the services you provide your child—laundry, cooking, grocery shopping, chauffeuring, and so on.

- Next, taking her age into consideration, decide which services she could do for herself.

- Then tell her, "Since you're not willing to do the chores you agreed to do, I've decided to do them. The chores will take some of my time, so I'll have to turn over to you some of the other things I do for you. If you're not willing to _____, then I'll do that, and you can do _____ instead." (Make sure that the tasks you are trading are equivalent and that those you are turning over are things you won't have to help with.)

- Finally, ask, "How do you feel about this?" If she complains, offer to negotiate as long as she is willing to stick to any agreement reached. If she won't negotiate or doesn't keep the new agreement, inform her that if she doesn't take care of the task, it will go undone.

- After a week, offer her a chance to renegotiate.

For task trading to be effective, you need a *good* relationship with your child in other areas. Chores are often a source of conflict and are not recommended as a starting place to change relationships. Don't use task trading as a weapon. The purpose is to teach mutual respect. Cooperation on chores is a measure of mutual respect in the family.

Some Considerations in Applying Logical Consequences

Logical consequences hold children accountable for their choices. A logical consequence

- shows mutual respect
- is firm and kind
- provides choices
- is concerned with what will happen now, not what happened in the past

- involves no moral judgment

- relates to the logic of the situation

- separates the deed from the doer*

When applying logical consequences, keep the following important points in mind:

1. *Identify the child's goal.* A natural consequence can be used with any of the four goals of misbehavior. You aren't involved; you're simply letting nature take its course. But when you devise logical consequences, it's important to consider the child's goal.

Logical consequences work best with attention-seekers, since conflict over this type of misbehavior is usually rather minor. When you notice attention-getting behavior that seems likely to be repeated, decide what consequences you'll use next time. Then let the child know what to expect.

When your child's goal is power or revenge, use logical consequences only when the behavior is truly disruptive and cannot be ignored. Children who display inadequacy aren't actively disruptive, so it's not necessary to use logical consequences with them. When children are not disruptive, it's better to work on building a positive relationship by using listening skills and encouragement.

2. *Recognize who owns the problem.* When your child owns the problem, it usually isn't necessary or desirable for you to devise consequences. Instead, step aside and give your child a chance to experience the consequences that will follow if you don't interfere. For example, if your son has his own library card, getting books back to the library on time is his responsibility. If his books are late, he will have to pay a fine. You don't need to get involved.

But if your son isn't doing his chores around the house, you're affected. You own the problem, and you will probably want to devise a logical consequence—for example, if it

---

*See the appendix for review material on natural and logical consequences.

Applying Assertive Skills

Situation	Possible Skills
Child plays stereo too loud.	*I-message:* "When the stereo is so loud, I get frustrated because I can't concentrate."
	Logical consequence: "Either turn the stereo down or turn it off. You decide."
Children complain about what is served for dinner.	*Logical consequence:* "I'm sorry, but that's what we have tonight. You can decide whether or not you want to eat."
	This could be followed by a *willingness statement:* "I'm willing to prepare some things you like to eat, if you're willing to help me plan menus before I go to the store."
Children of single parent complain because parent is going out on a date.	*Intention statement:* "I understand you don't like me going out. However, I have a right to some time with my friends. I do intend to go out tonight."
Child snacks in family room and leaves a mess.	*I-message:* "When I see crumbs and empty potato-chip bags all over the family room, I get discouraged because I worked hard cleaning the room. I'd appreciate it if you'd clean up when you're finished eating."
	Brief confrontation: "I have something that's been bothering me that I want to talk to you about. I want you to hear my feelings first, and then if you have something to say, I'll be glad to listen. When I find the family room full of crumbs and empty potato-chip bags, I feel discouraged because I spent a lot of time cleaning the room. If you're going to snack in the room, I want it cleaned up when you're finished."
	Logical consequence: "You can either clean up the family room when you're finished snacking, or stop snacking in there."
Teen and parent have a difference of opinion on how late the teen should stay out.	*Exploring alternatives:* "How can we work this out so we're both satisfied?"

has been decided that chores will be done on Saturday mornings, your son's other activities will wait until the chores are completed.

3. *Give choices that are logically related to the misbehavior and that are acceptable to both you and your child.*

Unlike punishment, which is arbitrary, logical consequences are related to the logic of the situation at hand. For example, suppose your daughter fails to put her dirty clothes in the laundry hamper. Refusing to wash them would be logically related to her misbehavior; refusing to allow her to go to the movies would not.

If you give choices with consequences your children are unwilling to accept, they may rebel. If you give choices with consequences you won't accept, you won't follow through.

4. *Accept and follow through on the child's choice.* Be prepared for your child to choose the consequence sometimes rather than stop the misbehavior. When this happens, simply follow through. Realize there are no wrong choices!

5. *Negotiate consequences when appropriate,* as will often be the case with older children and teens. Exploring alternatives is inappropriate if the misbehavior is either minor or so serious that choices are limited.

6. *Choose your words carefully;* be as brief as possible; and keep hostility out of your tone of voice and nonverbal behavior. When the child chooses the consequence, restate what you understand his or her choice to be: "I see you are choosing to . . ." Then avoid reminding and coaxing.

7. *Avoid hidden motives.* Consequences are not tricks to get your child to do what you want. Your long-term objective is cooperation. If your short-term objective is "This will show him!" you won't get the cooperation you seek. Children are smart—they can sense attempts to control or get even with them, no matter how well disguised.

8. After correcting misbehavior, look for positive behavior to comment on. *Catch your child being good.*

9. *Follow through in the future.* If your child chooses a consequence and then stops the misbehavior, all is well. But if the misbehavior is repeated, follow through consistently with the consequence, perhaps gradually increasing it in some way.

Conclusion

The procedures suggested in this chapter are based on mutual respect. That's the key to being firm and assertive without being autocratic. Aggressive, autocratic methods that try to control children will not teach self-discipline or instill a spirit of cooperation. But children usually do respond cooperatively if they sense that you accept and respect them as people.

When you give your children freedom to choose within the limits you set up, you communicate respect for them. When you remain firm in your decisions, you teach them to respect you. By doing both—using gentle strength and firm love—you give them the space and the structure they need to grow toward self-discipline.

Notes

1. Robert T. Bayard and Jean Bayard, *How to Deal with Your Acting-Up Teenager: Practical Self-Help for Desperate Parents* (New York: M. Evans and Co., 1981), 95. Used by permission of the authors.

2. Lee Schnebly, *Out of Apples: Lighthearted Psychology* (Tucson: Manzanas Press, 1984), 1.

3. Thomas Gordon, *Parent Effectiveness Training* (New York: Peter H. Wyden, 1970), 118.

Being an Effective Parent

This book has suggested ways of making the skills you learned in your *STEP* or *STEP/Teen* group part of your everyday family life. You've also gained new skills and have followed a systematic problem-solving process to address parenting challenges. This book can be a continuing reference and resource for you and your family.

As you practice what you've learned, maintain your self-esteem. Of course, you'll continue to make mistakes—not one of us is perfect. Furthermore, living together as a family is a continual learning experience for both parents and children—and learning is sometimes painful. But you have powerful tools to help you be the kind of parent you want to be. You understand that mutual respect is the key to successful parenting. You are an effective parent!

Family Enrichment Activity

Describe a discipline challenge you are facing with one of your children. Choose a challenge that has been especially difficult for you to meet. Take a few minutes to recall a specific incident and write down all the details you remember, telling exactly what your child did and said. Also describe what happened before and after the event.

_____

_____

_____

_____

_____

_____

_____

Ask yourself the following questions:

1. How did I feel about what happened? _____

_____

_____

_____

2. What did I say and do in response to the situation? _____

_____

_____

_____

3. What was I telling myself when this incident happened? ("It's not fair!" "I'll show him!") _____

_____

_____

_____

Family Enrichment Activity

4. What did my child do in response to my action? _____

_____

_____

_____

_____

5. What do I think my child's goal was in this interaction? _____

_____

6. What do the thoughts I was having during this incident tell me
about my beliefs? _____

_____

Are my beliefs interfering with my progress? _____
If so, how? _____

_____

_____

_____

7. Who owns the problem? _____

8. What will I do about the problem this week? _____

_____

_____

_____

_____

Points to Remember

1. Parents help their children become self-disciplined by using gentle strength and firm love.

2. Parents are responsible for maintaining control of the situation, not of the child.

3. We can set limits, but we can also allow choices within those limits.

4. Parents need to remain firm on limits set. To give in or fight is not love; it is disrespect.

5. Assertive parents stand up for their own rights. They calmly state what they are willing and not willing to do.

6. Taking time for yourself is a positive way to care for your family as well as yourself.

7. By communicating expectations in advance, parents help children live up to expectations.

8. Assertive parents use these skills:
   - I-messages, "I'd appreciate" statements, and statements of willingness and intention
   - brief confrontations
   - logical and natural consequences

Points to Remember

9. If there is difficulty getting the child to do chores, experiment with trading tasks.

10. When using logical consequences, parents need to
    - identify the child's goal
    - recognize who owns the problem
    - give choices the parent and the child are willing to accept
    - negotiate consequences
    - replace talk with action
    - monitor their tone of voice and nonverbal behavior
    - avoid hidden motives
    - follow through consistently with consequences if misbehavior continues

Appendix

Review of *STEP* Principles

This appendix contains brief summaries of the core concepts of *Systematic Training for Effective Parenting,* presented in the order in which they are discussed in *STEP* and *STEP/Teen:* goals of misbehavior, positive goals of behavior, family constellation, problem ownership, reflective listening, I-messages, and natural and logical consequences. For more detailed information on all these concepts, see *The Parent's Handbook* from *STEP* and *The Parent's Guide* from *STEP/Teen.*

The Goals of Misbehavior

Psychologists Alfred Adler and Rudolf Dreikurs believed that children behave the way they do because they are searching for a way to belong in the family. Children try out many types of behavior in their attempts to find some way to feel significant. They want

- to be loved and accepted
- to be secure
- to belong—to fit into a group
- to be approved and recognized for what they do
- to move toward independence, responsibility, and decision making

When children don't feel accepted, loved, secure, approved, and responsible, they get discouraged and are likely to misbehave.

Dreikurs believed that children misbehave in order to achieve one of the following goals: to get attention, power, or revenge, or to show that they feel inadequate.[1]

1. *Attention.* All children want attention, but some children seem to feel that they must be "center stage" in order to belong. They may misbehave because they prefer even negative attention to being ignored.

2. *Power.* Children in power struggles with their parents may argue, be defiant, or otherwise attempt to control the situation. Being able to get their own way allows them to feel significant.

3. *Revenge.* When power struggles are prolonged, children may come to feel that they cannot defeat their parents. Then they switch to the third goal, revenge. The revengeful child feels unlovable and hurt, and tries to find significance by hurting others in return.

4. *Display of Inadequacy.* If children suffer defeat too often while attempting to belong, they may give up and act helpless in an attempt to keep others from expecting anything of them.

Additional Goals. For teenagers, the list of goals can be extended to include excitement, superiority, and peer acceptance.

5. *Excitement.* Teens may pursue a goal of excitement by avoiding routine or showing an interest in alcohol, other drugs, sex, daredevil sports, fast driving.

6. *Superiority.* Teens who seek superiority may do so in destructive ways: by putting down parents and others, engaging in pointless or dangerous competition, or using their talents against others in some way.

7. *Peer acceptance.* Misbehavior sometimes results from wanting to conform and go along with the crowd, or being swept along by fads and fashions.

Determining the Goals of Misbehavior

To identify your child's goal of misbehavior, watch your reactions to the behavior and note how the child reacts to being corrected.

Attention
- You feel annoyed by what the child is doing.
- You are able to correct the behavior at least temporarily by reminding or coaxing. Later the child will

repeat the behavior or make a different bid for attention.

Power
- You feel angry and provoked.
- If you continue to fight, the child either struggles harder or does what you want in a defiant manner. If you give in or refuse to fight, the misbehavior stops.

Revenge
- You feel hurt and want to retaliate.
- If you retaliate, the child seeks further revenge.

Display of Inadequacy
- You feel despairing, hopeless, discouraged.
- Your attempts at correction fail or else the child responds passively. Eventually you give up, believing the child is truly unable to perform.

Excitement
- You feel shocked, surprised, nervous, angry, hurt, on your guard or on the defensive.
- If you intervene, the teen resists or continues the misbehavior.

Superiority
- You may feel approval and want to praise the teen, or you may feel inadequate and want to put the teen in his or her place.
- In response, the teen continues striving for superiority and continues putting down others to defend her or his own self-image.

Peer acceptance
- You feel approval if you agree with the teen's choice of friends; you feel worried and anxious if you disapprove.
- If you try to get the teen to seek new friends, he or she will resist or continue to see the friends you disapprove of. A power contest may result.

Dealing with Misbehavior after Determining Its Goal

Children and teens are usually not aware of having goals of misbehavior, and it will probably not be helpful to tell them what you think their goals are. Don't reward their misbehavior and their faulty goals by reacting in the ways they have come to expect. Make sure that your response takes into account their feelings of not belonging.

Attention. If you give children and teens attention when they misbehave, you reward their misbehavior. If you ignore their attention-seeking behavior whenever possible and instead notice and encourage positive behavior, they will be less likely to feel they need to misbehave to get your attention. But if you notice a "good" child using positive behavior simply to get attention, don't reward this negative goal. Work at giving attention when it is not expected. *A general guideline for responding to attention seeking is never to give attention on demand.*

Power. Trying to defeat children or teens in a power struggle only teaches them the importance of power. They may escalate the power struggle or push things further to see how much more they can get by with. If you win the power struggle, they may end up feeling more insignificant than ever. Refuse either to fight or to give in—it's better to look for a way to resolve the immediate situation than to demand obedience. *If you sidestep the power struggle and later enlist your child's cooperation by asking for help, opinions, and suggestions, she or he won't have anyone to rebel against.*

Revenge. Kindness and patience can help soften the desire for revenge. If you counterattack, your child will only seek further revenge, perhaps by intensifying the misbehavior. Instead, work to build a relationship based on trust. *Remember, children and teens who seek revenge desperately need love.*

Display of Inadequacy. Children and teens who feel inadequate need to know that they can succeed and belong and that they don't have to be perfect. Don't give up on them—remember, they're discouraged, not incompetent! *Avoid all criticism and provide lots of support and encouragement.*

Positive Goals of Behavior

Fortunately, behavior can have positive goals. Children who are confident that they belong want to cooperate and make a contribution to the group. Their goal is involvement and acceptance, rather than attention. Children who believe that they are responsible and able to make their own decisions have freedom and independence as their goals, rather than power. Children who believe that they are loved and lovable may strive for equal treatment of self and others rather than trying to "get even." Their goals are justice, cooperation, and equality. Children with healthy self-esteem may withdraw from conflict and power clashes, but for positive reasons—their goal is to settle things peacefully, not to avoid difficulty.

Stimulating Positive Goals

Parents can help children seek positive goals by
- focusing on effort and improvement
- taking note of any positive change
- listening for feelings, opinions, and ideas
- looking for assets and strengths to build on
- finding the positive in otherwise negative situations
- being sensitive to the child's interests
- valuing the child as a unique person and avoiding comparisons with siblings

Things you can do to encourage involvement, acceptance, and contribution:
- Appreciate the child's assistance and contributions. "I really appreciated your help. It made my job much easier."
- Provide opportunities for the child to make contributions.

- Plan ways to use the child's talents to contribute to the family on a continuing basis. Begin by listing the talents of each of your children.
- Invite the child to be involved in family activities.
- Accept and appreciate any attempts to contribute. "Thanks for helping."

To encourage freedom and independence:
- Provide opportunities for decision making and for taking responsibility. List the choices you can give each of your children.
- Express confidence in the child's decisions. "I know it's a challenge, but I have confidence in you." If necessary, remind the child of a past accomplishment: "Remember when you . . .?"
- Allow the child to take responsibility for the consequences of decisions—positive or negative.
- When appropriate, ask for and accept the child's help.

To encourage justice, cooperation, equality:
- Recognize the child's attempts to behave properly in social situations. "I noticed you decided that was not appropriate for you to do." "It looks like you're learning how to judge what's right for you and what's not."
- Stress equality in your relationship with the child. For example, don't expect children to do chores you don't want to do.
- Use family meetings to promote cooperation.
- Use family meetings to discuss values involving moral decisions. Avoid preaching. Respectfully discuss each point of view.

To encourage positive withdrawal:
- Recognize the child's attempts to withdraw from unproductive conflict.
- When conflicts develop, explore alternatives with the child to model positive ways to deal with conflict.
- Avoid becoming involved in sibling or peer conflicts.
- Refuse to fight with the child.
- Look for examples of solving conflicts positively. For example, watch television shows involving social conflicts. Then discuss with your child how the conflicts were resolved.

Family Constellation

The family constellation refers to the psychological position of each child in a family in relation to sisters and brothers. Each child in a family is born into a different set of circumstances: the firstborn in the family is an only child for a time, and then the oldest; any children born thereafter have to deal with an older and usually more advanced sibling. A child's psychological position in relation to siblings has a significant effect on psychological development. Constellation position is usually based on birth order, but that is not the sole determining factor—a child's position also depends on how the child sees herself or himself in relation to siblings.

Some typical characteristics of each family position are shown in the chart that follows. Keep in mind that the traits listed are only possibilities. Not all children will have the characteristics listed. Some children will have characteristics which overlap with other positions due to other influences, such as age differences and culture.

Some Typical Characteristics of Family Constellation Positions

Position	Strives to	Possible Positive Traits	Possible Negative Traits
Only Child	Get own way (may play "divide and conquer")	• Is creative* • Has positive peer relationships as an adult** • Is selective about choosing whom to please	• May be pampered and spoiled, or self-centered • Feels incompetent — feels adults are more capable • Relies on service from others rather than being self-reliant
Oldest Child	Be first	• Is a leader • Is helpful and responsible • Is competent	• Is bossy • Believes *must* please others • Becomes discouraged if can't be the best (may become the "first worst")
Second Child	Catch up or overtake	• Is sociable • Puts forth effort • Develops abilities lacking in the oldest	• May rebel • Can become "bad" child if oldest is the "good" child • Is uncertain of abilities if the oldest child is successful
Middle Child of Three***	Make life fair	• Is adaptable • Is concerned with justice • Knows how to get along with all kinds of people	• Feels "squeezed" — may push others down to elevate self • May be a "problem" child • Feels doesn't have a place
Youngest Child	Get service	• Knows how to influence others • Is charming • Is friendly	• May be manipulative • Expects others to take care of his or her responsibilities • Feels inferior or overtakes older siblings

*Only children may have to learn how to operate in a world made up exclusively of adults and may have to entertain themselves. This may develop their creative side.

**When they are growing up, only children may want to be adults and may have poor peer relationships as a result. When they become adults, they often believe they've finally "made it" and can now relate better to adults as peers.

***Middle children in a large family don't compete as much as middles of three, since their parents don't have as much time to reinforce the competition. Therefore, middle children from large families are usually more cooperative.

Problem Ownership

In trying to decide how to respond to your child's misbehavior, it's helpful to keep in mind that a response is not always necessary. Some parents feel they must be involved in all aspects of their children's lives. But some problems actually "belong" to children. Of course, a three-year-old may need help coping with a problem that a six-year-old could be left to solve independently. And, no matter what a child's age, there are many times when parents will *want* to help, or at least lend an ear. Yet parents will find there are still many problems children can handle by themselves.

Children need to have a chance to own their own problems and search for their own solutions. Sometimes they need to make their own mistakes without any interference from their parents. They need to learn that we all have a responsibility to solve our own problems.

Here are the possibilities to be considered when determining who owns a problem:

- For some reason the child is not getting what he or she wants. But this creates no difficulties for you. The child owns the problem.
- The child is getting what she or he wants. However, the child's behavior is interfering with your rights or responsibilities; perhaps someone's safety is at stake. Therefore, you own the problem.
- The child is getting what he or she wants. The child's behavior is not interfering with you. Therefore, there is no problem in the parent-child relationship.
- Your child is in conflict with someone else—a teacher, a friend, your spouse. The problem is between them, and—dangerous situations excepted—it's probably better for you not to get involved.[2]

Reflective Listening

Reflective listening is a special listening skill that you can use to show children—and adults too—that you understand what they are thinking or feeling. With reflective listening you reflect, like a mirror, what you see or hear the other person saying. The easiest way to present the feeling you're hearing is to use the words "You feel," followed by "because": "You feel hurt because your sister ignored you." The purpose of a reflective listening response is to let a person know that she or he is being heard.[3]

I-Messages

Speaking with I-messages, rather than you-messages, is an effective way of making yourself heard. You-messages put people down—they label and lay blame: "You and your mess—I'm sick and tired of picking up after you." People on the receiving end of a you-message usually don't feel much like cooperating with the person sending it. I-messages, on the other hand, set the stage for cooperation. I-messages respectfully share how you feel about the consequences someone's behavior creates for you.

I-messages come in three parts: *When . . . I feel . . . because.* "When the den's a mess, I feel discouraged, because it's not pleasant to be in here!"

You can vary the "When, I feel, because" sequence. What's important is to state the problem and tell how you feel about it and why, and to do this in a respectful way, without criticizing or blaming.[4]

Natural and Logical Consequences

All behavior has consequences. Consequences result from the choices we make and the actions we take. Allowing your children to experience the consequences of their behavior can help them learn valuable lessons about the way the world works. It also emphasizes that their behavior is their own responsibility.

Natural Consequences. If you go out in the rain without a raincoat or umbrella, you'll get wet. If you skip a meal, you'll get hungry. If you stay up late and have to get up early, you'll feel tired. In these examples, getting wet, hungry, and tired are the natural consequences of your behavior, consequences imposed by the laws of nature, not by other people. The same consequence occurs for an adult as for a child. Allowing natural consequences of behavior to occur is often more effective than a parent's intervention because such consequences are impersonal. The child sees a clearcut connection between the behavior and its results.

You may be reluctant to allow your child to experience natural consequences. It's natural to feel protective of your children. But if you "let nature take its course" whenever it's safe to do so, your children will quickly learn the responsible behavior necessary to avoid natural consequences.

Logical Consequences. Logical consequences are the result of going against rules of social cooperation. For example, if you're late for your bus or plane, it will leave without you. If you don't pay your electric bill, your service may be disconnected. The bus driver or electric company isn't punishing you. They are simply letting you take the logical consequences of your chosen action.

Children's misbehavior often has built-in logical consequences. If Emily doesn't pay attention in school, or doesn't finish her homework, she'll get a low grade. If Timmy fights with Cliff, Cliff may not want to play with him.

This idea can be carried into the area of parental discipline. When parents need to intervene to stop misbehavior, they can devise their own logical consequences.

Like natural consequences, logical consequences don't involve moral judgments or putdowns, and they have a clear relationship to the misbehavior. They are designed to fit the specific situation. For example, a teen who borrows the family car and returns it with the gas gauge sitting on "empty" could lose the privilege of using the car for a specific period of time.

Logical consequences should be explained in a way that emphasizes mutual rights and mutual respect. They aren't to be used as threats. It works best to apply them kindly and firmly. A logical consequence must be perceived as logical by the child. In fact, it helps to involve the child in deciding what the consequences of problem behavior will be.

In applying logical consequences, always provide choices. This will help remind children that they have a choice about how they behave. Propose alternatives for the child and then accept the child's decision, pointing out that there will be an opportunity to change the decision later. Use a friendly tone of voice, one that reflects an attitude of good will and a sense of caring. The respect, acceptance, and understanding you communicate will help to create a feeling of belonging.[5]

Notes

1. Rudolf Dreikurs and Vicki Soltz, *Children: The Challenge* (New York: Hawthorn, 1964).
2. Thomas Gordon, *Parent Effectiveness Training* (New York: Peter H. Wyden, 1970).
3. Robert R. Carkhuff, David H. Berenson, and Richard M. Pierce, *The Skills of Teaching: Interpersonal Skills* (Amherst, Mass.: Human Resource Development Press, 1977).
4. Gordon, 1970.
5. Dreikurs and Soltz, 1964.

Group Discussion Programs—More Help for Becoming an Effective Parent

- *STEP*—for parents of preschool through middle-school children (also available in a Spanish-language edition, *PECES [Padres Eficaces Con Entrenamiento Sistemático])*
- *STEP/Teen*—for parents of junior-high and high-school youth
- *The Next STEP*—a follow-up program based on this book, *The Effective Parent*—for parents who wish to extend the skills taught in *STEP* and *STEP/Teen*

Why Join a Group Discussion Program?

Over 1,500,000 parents have participated in *STEP, STEP/Teen,* and *The Next STEP.* These parents report
- increased knowledge of parenting
- improved relationships in their families
- improved communication with their children
- less conflict in the family

In one study, *over 93%* of *STEP* "graduates" said they would recommend the course to other parents.

What makes *STEP* programs so effective? Group support! Participants learn and practice new skills in an atmosphere of mutual support, cooperation, and open communication. They meet other parents who face similar challenges and share their concerns. Everyone has the opportunity to give and receive encouragement and share insights and solutions.

Which Group Should You Select?

If you've completed a *STEP* or *STEP/Teen* course, you'll want to enroll in *The Next STEP.* You'll extend your *STEP* skills and learn new concepts and techniques to further improve your family relationships.

If you're new to *STEP,* we recommend you begin by taking *STEP* or *STEP/Teen*—depending on the ages of your children. If you want to take *The Next STEP* first, talk with the course leader when you sign up about ways to prepare.

Groups in Your Community

If you are interested in joining, or leading, a *STEP, STEP/Teen,* or *Next STEP* group, there are many organizations in your community that might be able to give you information. Check to see whether groups are being offered by local schools, community centers, health centers, churches and synagogues, adult education programs, counseling centers, civic groups, psychologists, social workers, or the military.

For additional details about *STEP, STEP/Teen, The Next STEP,* or *PECES* groups in your area, or for information about how to start a group yourself, write to the publisher:

AGS®
American Guidance Service
Publishers' Building
Circle Pines, MN 55014-1796

In Canada, write to:
Psycan Corporation
160 West Beaver Creek Road
Unit 5
Richmond Hill, Ontario
L4B 1B4

In Australia, write to:
Australian Council for Educational Research Ltd.
P.O. Box 210
Hawthorn, Victoria 3122

To learn about other family-support publications, including
- *TIME—Training in Marriage Enrichment*
- *PREP for Effective Family Living*
- *Strengthening Stepfamilies*
- *Responsive Parenting*
- *Aging: A New Look*

write to AGS at the address above.

SKILL CARD 1
Steps of Group Problem Solving

1. Present your parenting problem to the group:

- Tell what your child did and how you felt about it.
- Explain what you said and did in response to the child's behavior.
- Tell what your thoughts were.
- Describe what the child did in response to your words and action.

2. Let group members guess what the child's goal of misbehavior was.

(over)

SKILL CARD 2
A Self-Affirmation Exercise

This exercise becomes more effective with practice. Read through the instructions before you begin.

- Close your eyes and take several deep breaths to relax your body.
- Picture yourself sitting in a chair about four feet away.
- Think of a quality you want to possess. Now picture yourself having that quality.
- Believe that this quality is yours. Claim it for yourself and act as if you already possess it.
- Open your eyes.

SKILL CARD 3
How Family Members Can Nourish Self-Esteem

- Show you love and value one another.
- Allow for individual differences.
- Appreciate uniqueness.
- Communicate openly.
- Look for opportunities to be encouraging.
- Keep your sense of humor.
- Recognize that it's okay to make mistakes.
- Find ways to support one another.
- Share responsibilities.

SKILL CARD 4
Self-Affirmation Statements

Experiment with saying self-affirming things to yourself, either out loud or silently. Set aside time to practice this while looking in a mirror. Repeat self-affirmations while you are showering, jogging, driving to work, or simply taking time to relax. Here are some examples:

- I make decisions for myself.
- I'm a responsible person.
- I like who I am.
- I can see what's positive in any situation.
- I can see possibilities and alternatives.

(over)

SKILL CARD 5
Ways to Encourage Yourself

- Look for possibilities and solutions, not threats and dangers.
- Consciously choose how you interpret events and come up with constructive ways of looking at situations.
- Keep your sense of humor and see things in perspective.
- Make a choice and take responsibility for it, believing that what happens to you is a result of the choices you make.
- Focus on your strengths and realize that it's not necessary to compare yourself to others.
- Enjoy your accomplishments.

(over)

SKILL CARD 6
Ways to Build Your Child's Self-Esteem

- Give feedback that makes a clear distinction between the behavior and the person. Let your actions communicate "I may not like what you are doing, but I still love you."
- Encourage independence: "I know you can solve that by yourself."
- Give responsibility and expect cooperation: "I'll take care of the laundry if you'll put your dirty clothes in the hamper."
- Accept mistakes. In school-work, instead of focusing on errors, encourage the child:

(over)

SKILL CARD 7
Building Self-Esteem as a Couple

Here are guidelines for an activity many couples have found helpful:

1. Sit down facing each other in a quiet, private place. You may want to hold hands.

2. Tell your partner, "The most positive thing that happened today was . . ." Then go on to say, "Something I appreciated about you today was . . ." Take three to five minutes.

3. Ask your partner to feed back the ideas, beliefs, feelings, or values she or he has heard.

4. While your partner takes three

(over)

SKILL CARD 8
Developing the Positive Side of the Personality Priorities

Superiority
- Give your children responsibility, expect them to contribute, let them own their own problems.
- Nourish their self-esteem: believe in them, respect them, appreciate them.

Control
- Focus on controlling the situation, not the child. Give choices within the guidelines you provide.

(over)

SKILL CARD 9
Some Irrational Beliefs

1. It is necessary to be loved and approved of by everyone.

2. I must be thoroughly competent in every respect and a high achiever in all areas.

3. My unhappiness is caused by outside forces that I have little control over.

4. When things are not the way I would like them to be, it's a catastrophe.

5. It is easier to avoid life's difficulties and responsibilities than to face them.

6. I have to worry about other people's problems.

(over)

3. Ask the group if they have spotted any mistaken beliefs on your part that may be interfering with your effectiveness.

4. With the help of the group, identify who owns the problem.

5. Brainstorm different ways of looking at the situation.

6. Continue brainstorming to find suggestions for improving the parent-child relationship.

7. Choose a specific course of action, explain why you chose it, and make a commitment to stick with it until the next session.

"Look how many answers you got right!" You may want to show that you accept mistakes by not commenting on them at all.
- Encourage your child to see the humorous side of events: "I like your sense of humor." Show you can laugh at yourself. Take care never to appear to be laughing at your child.
- Encourage self-appreciation: "You sound pleased with your work."
- Accept and value the child's uniqueness: "You're very imaginative."
- Be positive:
  "I'll bet we can figure out a solution. What ideas do you have?"

AGS*

---

7. I should never make mistakes with my children.

8. My children are to blame for my anger, anxiety, and frustration.

9. My children must be perfect: they should never make mistakes or be in a bad mood; they should always be well-behaved and competent.

10. I must criticize, nag, scold, lecture, and act hostile toward my children in order to get them to cooperate.

11. If my child behaves differently than I had hoped, this proves I am a failure as a parent.

AGS*

- Avoid negative self-talk:
  "I can't get it done."
  "My kids aren't cooperative."
  "It's impossible."

AGS*

- Involve your older children in deciding what a situation requires and in setting limits and consequences.

Pleasing
- Be firm as well as kind when you encounter a situation requiring consequences.
- Take care of yourself and don't spend all your time trying to satisfy others.

Comfort
- Be willing to sacrifice your comfort to your children's wishes at least some of the time.
- Let your children take care of their own comfort.

AGS*

- I'm encouraging to others.
- I'm capable and effective in my work.
- I'm worthwhile.

AGS*

---

to five minutes to complete those same sentences, listen attentively and do not interrupt. Maintain eye contact.

5. Feed back to your partner what you have heard.

Additional topics that can be used in the same format are
"The most enjoyable thing I did this week was . . ."
"Something I enjoy about you is . . ."
"Something I'm looking forward to doing with you is . . ."*

---

*Don Dinkmeyer and Jon Carlson, *Time for a Better Marriage* (Circle Pines, Minn.: American Guidance Service, 1984), 27.

AGS*

SKILL CARD 10
Deep Breathing Exercise

Find a quiet place where you will not be disturbed. Sit in a comfortable chair, preferably one with a straight back. Take off your shoes. Sit back in the chair. Breathe in and out, slowly and deeply, but naturally. Breathe deeply into your abdomen, so that your stomach swells each time you inhale. Say the word *relax* each time you breathe out. As you breathe in and out, slowly, deeply, and naturally, you will begin to feel tension drain from your body.

(over)

SKILL CARD 11
Muscle Relaxation Exercise

Begin by making a tight fist. You should feel tension in your hand, over your knuckles, and in your lower arm. Hold the level of tension for five to seven seconds, counting to yourself. Then quickly release the tension. Be sure to release it abruptly, not gradually. Pay close attention to the physical sensations associated with tensing and then relaxing a muscle group, so that you will know what deep relaxation feels like.

Next, tense and then relax your other hand and forearm. One by

(over)

SKILL CARD 12
"The Relaxation Response"

It is easiest to do this exercise in a quiet, calm environment.

1. Sit quietly in a comfortable position.

2. Close your eyes.

3. Deeply relax all your muscles, beginning at your feet and progressing up to your face. Keep them relaxed.

4. Breathe through your nose. Become aware of your breathing. As you breathe out, say the word "ONE" silently to yourself.... Breathe easily and naturally.

(over)

SKILL CARD 13
Using Visual Imagery to Relax

First, relax by concentrating on your breathing. Deeply inhale and exhale. Visualize the strengthening energies of life traveling into your body and filling your lungs as you inhale. Then envision undesirable emotions and difficulties leaving your body as you exhale.

Choose an image that is meaningful to you, one that suggests peace, strength, or a calm, quiet happiness. A mountain, a pool of water, or the ocean are images some people associate with se-

(over)

SKILL CARD 14
A Format for Family Meetings

Many families who prefer a formal approach to family meetings find that the following format works well:

1. Read and discuss the minutes of the previous meeting.

2. Discuss any issues left unresolved last time.

3. Consider each new item on the agenda.

4. After discussing as many agenda items as time allows, summarize the meeting by reviewing decisions, agreements,

(over)

SKILL CARD 15
Exploring Alternatives at Family Meetings

Exploring alternatives is a good way to solve problems at family meetings. These are the steps:

1. Understand and clarify the problem.

2. Explore alternatives through brainstorming.

3. Evaluate proposed alternatives.

4. Choose a solution.

5. Make a commitment and set a time to evaluate.

SKILL CARD 16
Using Logical Consequences Appropriately

Here are six principles for using consequences appropriately:

1. Don't use a logical consequence when a safe natural consequence exists.

2. Make sure your consequences are logical to the child.

3. Make sure the consequence is directly related to the misbehavior and reflects the needs of the situation.

4. Accept the child's decision and follow through.

(over)

SKILL CARD 17
Things to Consider When Consequences Fail

If you experience problems with consequences, ask yourself the following questions:

1. Were logical consequences appropriate for this problem? Would another skill have been more appropriate in this situation?

2. Was the action logical and appropriate for the misbehavior?

3. Did the consequence reflect the needs of the situation?

4. Was my timing appropriate?

(over)

SKILL CARD 18
Some Considerations in Applying Logical Consequences

1. Identify the child's goal.

2. Recognize who owns the problem.

3. Give choices that are logically related to the misbehavior and that are acceptable to both you and your child.

4. Accept and follow through on the child's choice.

5. Negotiate consequences when appropriate.

6. Choose your words carefully.

7. Avoid hidden motives.

(over)

5. Continue for 10-20 minutes. You may open your eyes to check the time, but do not use an alarm. When you finish, sit quietly for several minutes, at first with your eyes closed and later with your eyes opened.

6. Do not worry about whether you are successful in achieving a deep level of relaxation. Maintain a passive attitude and permit relaxation to occur at its own pace. When distracting thoughts occur, try to ignore them by not dwelling upon them and return to repeating "ONE." *

———
*Herbert Benson, *The Relaxation Response* (New York: William Morrow, 1975).

AGS®

---

one, tense and then relax the other major muscle groups in the body: biceps (front muscle, upper arm), triceps (back muscle, upper arm), head area (eyes, face, throat), shoulder muscles, upper back muscles, lower back muscles, chest muscles, stomach muscles, pelvic muscles, buttocks, upper leg muscles, calf and shin muscles, feet and toes.

With each set of muscles, hold the tension five to seven seconds, notice how the tension feels, and then quickly release it. Feel the muscle deeply relax.*

———
*Edmund Jacobson, *You Must Relax* (New York: McGraw Hill, 1962).

AGS®

The Quieting Response

Here's a simplified version of QR you can use:

1. Smile inwardly and give yourself the suggestion, "alert mind — calm body."

2. Inhale easily, taking a deep breath.

3. While exhaling, let jaw, tongue, and shoulders go limp, feeling a wave of heaviness and warmth flow to the toes.

4. Resume normal activity.*

———
*Charles F. Stroebel, *Quieting Reflex Training for Adults,* available from BMA Audiocassette Publications, 200 Park Ave. S., New York, NY 10003. Sound cassette.

AGS®

---

and commitments. Then evaluate the meeting by asking members how they feel about the decisions reached.

5. Agree on a time for the next meeting.

---

renity and peace. Now visualize the image "in your mind's eye" with as much detail as possible. Begin to feel the qualities you associate with the image. Hold onto these feelings for as long as you can before emerging from your state of relaxation.

---

8. Catch your child being good.
9. Follow through in the future.

AGS®

---

5. Was I using consequences as another form of punishment, or was it really my intention to let my child learn from experience?

6. Was I kind as well as firm?

7. Did I use action or did I talk too much?

8. Did I establish mutual respect with my child? Did I reject the behavior, but still accept the child?

9. Were my actions hostile or matter-of-fact?

10. Am I spending enough time encouraging positive behavior, as well as trying to correct misbehavior?

AGS®

---

5. When possible, involve the child in constructing the consequence.

6. When the child misbehaves and so chooses the consequence, keep talking to a minimum. Replace talk with action.

AGS®